What peop

MW01614970

"Katharine, I received the manual the day after I ordered it which was great because I was anxious to get it. Once I picked it up, I could not put it down until I finished. I was extremely pleased and excited about the contents of the manual. You thought of everything! Now thanks to you I have a more focused vision of what I want to do and how to go about getting there. It is definitely the ONLY manual I would and have already recommended for those thinking about starting a concierge service. Thank you for providing such an excellent and thorough source of information for those of us struggling to find material for this business."

Ineavelle Middleton
Middco Go-For Services
Greensboro, NC

"I have read your manual on starting your own concierge business. Let me tell you - It was wonderful. The examples and all of the tried and true advice made sense. I have read too many home business books that are too general, even if the table of contents suggests otherwise. As a result I am working on my business plan and have developed a name "Spirit Concierge" which I intend to register within the next week. So thank you for putting together exactly what I needed. Thanks again for a wonderfully written "How to..." guide. It made it easy to get started."

Carla Mandell
Spirit Concierge
Philadelphia, PA

"I received my manual—and I am well pleased! It is full of vital information, some things I never considered or thought of. Thank you again for writing such a well informed manual."

Joyce Thomas
The 5th Avenue Concierge

"Purchasing your manual and contracts has been by far, the best investment we have made into our business! Thank you so much for the invaluable information and all the support you have given us! It is nice to know there still is service after the sale."

Steven & Michelle
MidWest Concierge

"The books are excellent and have assisted my progress immensely. Thank you!"

Blue Star Concierge Services
Sydney, Australia

"I just finished reading your step by step guide and I would like to thank you for the invaluable information you've provided to those of us just getting started in this business."

Classic Concierge
Phoenix, Arizona

The Concierge Manual

A Step by Step Guide on How to Start your own Concierge and/or Errand Service

Katharine C. Giovanni

good Luck!

Katharine Giovanni

NewRoad Publishing   Apex, NC

The Concierge Manual
A Step by Step Guide on How to start your own Concierge and/or Errand Service

Published By:

NewRoad Publishing
PO Box 278
Apex, NC 27502
Email: info@newroadpublishing.com
Website: www.newroadpublishing.com

All rights reserved. No part of this book can be reproduced or transmitted in any form or by any means, electronic or mechanical, including photocopying, recording or by any information storage and retrieval system without written permission of the author.

All rights reserved
Copyright 1999, 2000 by Katharine C. Giovanni

An application to register this book for cataloging has been submitted to the Library of Congress.

ISBN 1-931109-00-1

Printed in the United States of America by Jostens

To Ron

For without his love, support and wisdom
this book would never have been possible

And to my Mother

Her incredible strength, courage and dignity taught me to
never give up no matter what the obstacle. She proved that
you can keep walking towards the light
one day at a time ... no matter what.

Thanks Mom, you are missed.

Ambition

So many worlds, so much to do,
So little done, such things to be.

Lord Tennyson (1809–92),

Here are some questions that this manual will answer...

1. What skills do I need to become a successful concierge?
2. How do I get started? What do I need to do?
3. Do I need insurance?
4. What kind of database and software do I need?
5. Do I need a website? How do I get one?
6. What kind of services should I offer?
7. Do I need any contracts for liability issues?
8. How do I set my fees?
9. How much should I charge?
10. How is the Client going to pay for the services?
11. What are the logistics of actually running the errand? How do I do it?
12. What are service vendors?
13. Can I obtain a commission? Who will give me one?
14. Where do I find them?
15. How do I set up the errand service?
16. Where do I find the drivers?
17. Should they be independent contractors or employees?
18. How do I hire a staff? What kind of things should I look for?
19. Should I add meeting and event planning to my list of services?
20. Do you have any meeting and event planning tips?
21. How do I sell and market my new business?
22. Should I send out a press release?

Achievement

There are two great rules in life, the one general and the other particular. The first is that every one can in the end get what he wants if he only tries. This is the general rule. The particular rule is that every individual is more or less of an exception to the general rule.

Samuel Butler (1835–1902)

Table of Contents

Chapter 5 - Website Creation Made Easy

Chapter 6 - Setting up your Services

Chapter 7 - Fee Setting

Chapter 8 - Logistics

Chapter 9 - Service Vendors and Commissions

Chapter 10 - Errand Service

Chapter 11 - Staff

Chapter 12 - Meeting and Event Planning

Chapter 13 - Sales and Marketing

Chapter 14 - 30 Ways to grow your business   159

Chapter 15 - The Media   167

Chapter 16 - Bibliography   175

Warning — Disclaimer

The content of this manual is intended to be informational only. This manual is not, and should not be considered to be, presenting you with any type of business opportunity offering or its equivalent. The content of this manual is not intended to represent to you that you can operate a concierge business profitably, or that the estimates regarding costs, projected income or any other financial projections will prove to be accurate in your area, or based upon your efforts. Ultimately, any financial projections, estimates, etc. are based upon factors beyond the control of the author. This manual is intended to provide you with factual assistance regarding the concierge industry and should be understood as such.

Every effort has been made to make this manual as complete as possible, however, there may be mistakes, both typographical and in content. Therefore, this manual should be used only as a general guide and not as the ultimate source of concierge information.

The author and NewRoad Publishing shall have neither liability nor responsibility to any person or entity with respect to any loss or damage caused, or alleged to have been caused, directly or indirectly, by the information contained in this book.

If you do not wish to be bound by the above information, you may return this book to NewRoad Publishing for a full refund.

Acknowledgements

Many special thanks go to my husband and business partner, Ron Giovanni, for all the help, love, wisdom and support he gave me in putting together this book.

Nicole Perrin-Grizzard of Go-Fers Unlimited, Inc. for her friendship and invaluable help and support in putting together this book. It would not have not been possible without her assistance. Friends like this are rare - Thanks Nikki!

Many thanks also go to:

Brian Azar of the Sales Catalyst for both his extraordinary friendship and his wisdom in pushing me forward.

Becky Cross Saganich for her incredible friendship, support and wisdom in moving me to write the book in the first place, as well as for editing the original manuscript.

Sherie and Bryan Simpson for their support and friendship.

Doug and Polly Johns of Phoenix Environmental Services in North Carolina for teaching me about customer service and for providing such a wonderful example for all of us to follow.

Cheryl McGraw of Jostens for her invaluable help and patience.

And last but certainly not least my thanks go to my brother Jarvis Cromwell and my sister-in-law Shelby for all their love and support through the years.

Thank you everyone!

This book could not have been written if it wasn't for all of you. You have my most sincere thanks.

Success

Choose your success with all the conviction and determination that you can muster. Be clear in your choosing then feel the decision and move forward.

Feel the power of a bulldozer with the love and grace of an angels touch

Choose the path that you intend to see come through and make it happen.

Katharine Giovanni

Foreward

I have been a meeting and event planner for over 15 years and
have set up two successful businesses: Meeting Planning Plus
and Triangle Concierge. After graduating with a B.A. from
Lake Forest College in 1984, I began my career by working for
the American Society of Corporate Secretaries from 1986 until
1994. ASCS is a society whose members include Corporate
Secretaries, CEO's and Treasurers of the major Fortune 500
companies around the country.

While at ASCS I was responsible for organizing and
implementing corporate conferences, seminars, board/
committee meetings, exhibits, and banquets across the United
States and in Canada.   The conferences I organized included
banquets, tours, spouse programs, educational programs, as
well as children's programs. I chose the site, developed
program logistics, arranged ground transportation, selected
speakers and provided clients with written materials that
included brochures and conference materials.

I was also the official "gopher" for all those VIP's doing
whatever they needed done. Whether it was meeting them at
the airport, doing an errand, getting them some lunch or
having their handouts copied and collated. In fact, more often
than not I was the one adding a last minute item to all those
attendee workbooks.

Isn't this beginning to sound like concierge work? Remember
that in those days there was no such thing as a corporate
concierge so when someone needed work of this sort done they

called a meeting planner. Meeting planners are very used to wearing 30 hats while doing a balancing act on the high wire. No request is too outrageous for the planner because she/he becomes very adept at finding the hard to find and doing the impossible. Catering to the needs of VIP's, speakers, meeting attendees, co-workers and even family is what a meeting planner does. Today, that same individual can also be called a "concierge".

Working for ASCS proved invaluable for establishing my own business. My experience gave me the foundation I needed in dealing with the officers of the corporate world. Never underestimate how important that understanding is. It can make or break a contract.

My husband and I started Meeting Planning Plus in 1995. Over the years, we began to realize that we were doing much more concierge-type work than meeting planning. We also learned that the concierge services industry had the potential for taking off and was fast becoming the wave of the future. So after a few modifications, we changed our company name and targeted concierge services. Triangle Concierge was born in the fall of 1998.

As I began Triangle Concierge it soon became apparent that there were no resource materials available on the market to help me get started. There were no books on the subject or consultants to approach. Frankly I was unable to locate any helpful information. I was on my own. It took me approximately a year to teach myself and research how to start a concierge service (truly the ultimate of self-taught) and we were ready to open for business.

Almost immediately the telephone started to ring. First one call, then ten. People started calling and emailing me from all over the world asking me to spare just a moment of my time to tell them how I started my business, and I told them. I spent hours answering each question as best as I could. Until one day my husband overheard me and asked me what I was doing. When I told him he said, "why are you doing it for free?" Good question! Why indeed was I?

So, based on my expertise in meeting planning, concierge work, and the fact that I had started two successful companies I decided to write a manual on how to start your own concierge business. Just because I learned everything the hard way doesn't mean that others have to. There was most certainly a huge need for the information because in those early days there was no information at all. Anywhere.

I spent the next 8 weeks or so writing the first edition of the Concierge Manual. Once the book began to sell, the phone calls increased dramatically in a matter of weeks. I received calls and emails from all over the world from people wanting more services and information, asking questions and the like. As a result of all this we realized that we had to make a decision regarding our company's focus.

At the time, I was spending 90% of my time consulting, and 10% trying to grow my local concierge business. So, after a long discussion, in 1999 Triangle Concierge International, the concierge consultants, was born. We officially turned ourselves into full time concierge consultants and let go of our local concierge business.

The materials that I developed for the original Triangle Concierge are now being shared with the world through this book. The information, forms, brochures, sales letters, proposals and all the information that I learned over the past 15 years has gone into these pages so that others do not have to make the same mistakes that I did.

Today, I've consulted with companies and individuals from all over the world including Australia, England, Norway, Holland, The Netherlands, Germany, Canada, New Zealand, Spain and the United States to name a few. Triangle Concierge was one of the first two companies in the world to do concierge consulting. More have actually popped up since the publication of our first edition in 1998. Medical and legal professionals have been specializing for years – we just did the same thing.

It is my ultimate hope that the ideas that are presented here will help you set up your own business. Since there are about 10,001 ways to set up a concierge business, some of the opinions presented in this book will help you, and some will not. Review the entire manual, use those ideas that work for you and discard the ones that don't. Owning your own business is hard work, but it can be very rewarding and is never dull.

So my advice is to take it one day at a time and to not lose your focus. Stay focused on what you are doing and where you would like to go. If you find yourself getting discouraged because the clients are not coming as fast as you would like, take heart because persistence is the key to this business. Assume that your business is going to soar! Do not say you are going to just give it a try ... simply do it and make it happen. If you assume that your business is going to be a HUGE success, and you think this thought with every bone in your body, then it will. You will run into obstacles along the way of course, but assume that these too will work themselves out and somehow they will.

I have been an entrepreneur for many years now, and I can tell you from personal experience that it has not always been an easy road, but it has definitely been worth it and I would do it again in a heartbeat. Being your own boss without having to deal with rush hour traffic, office politics, misunderstandings with your boss, and never having to wonder if the sludge on the bottom of the coffee pot is drinkable is wonderful! Tell me, where else can you go to work in your bathrobe?

Simply make the choice to be a success and you will. Feel the decision and move forward. Feel the power of a bulldozer with the love and grace of an angels touch. You can do it, I know you can! Good luck!

Katharine C. Giovanni

Persistence

"Nothing in the world can take the place of persistence.

Talent will not; nothing is more common than
unsuccessful men with talent.

Genius will not; unrewarded genius is almost a proverb.

Education will not; the world is full of educated derelicts.

Persistence and determination alone are omnipotent."

Calvin Coolidge

Introduction

The concierge business is growing by leaps and bounds, and concierge companies are literally popping up all over corporate America. Concierge services have been available for some time but were historically only found in hotel lobbies. Recently, however, these services have begun to emerge in the corporate world.

Many companies located in cities such as Washington, Chicago and Boston have not only started to use corporate concierges but also are making them a part of their corporate benefit packages. They are reasoning correctly that the less time people spend running personal errands during the workday, the more time they can spend at their desks and subsequently with their families at night.

We all have to do a balancing act every day, and although everyone's is different, many go something like this ...

Once you get breakfast on the table, pack the lunches and get the children off to school, you rush off to work only to get slammed by rush hour traffic. At lunch you make some personal telephone calls, run to the drug store, dry cleaners, buy your son a new knapsack for school and quickly return the video you rented last week. Then you grab a fast-food sandwich on the way back to work. Sound familiar yet?

After work you pick up the kids, take them to their various after-school activities, make dinner, and afterwards make appointments at the doctor, dentist and the vet. Then you make some more telephone calls, a golf tee time for next weekend because your father-in-law is coming, and take the groceries and prescription you purchased after work over to your elderly mother's house. You then put her groceries away, tidy up her house, feed the cat, walk the dog and make her a quick meal.

Tired yet? Wouldn't it be great to have a personal assistant who could do this stuff for you? An affordable one?

Most people, unfortunately, do not have their own assistants so they try to cram these little errands into their after-work hours and already busy Saturdays. More often than not, however, they creep into regular work time. After all, most people who you need to do business with do business during regular work hours right?

In fact, sometimes it just seems like there isn't enough hours in the day. We are simply exhausted from the increasing demands placed on us at work and the daily commute, and at the end of the day we drag ourselves home to give only sleepy-eyed attention to our families.

According to a recent study of the U.S. work force released by the Families and Work Institute (statistics found online at www.entrepreneurmag.com):

- The average worker spends 44 hours per week on the job
- 36 % of workers say they often feel completely used up at the end of the workday.
- 85% of workers have daily family responsibilities to go home to.
- 78% of married workers have spouses who are also employed.
- Weekends are consumed by errands and housekeeping.
- 70% of all parents feel that they don't spend enough time with their children.

Down time? What's that? No one has the time for it anymore.

When looking at these statistics it is easy to see why time has become the commodity of the '90s and will be even more so in the next century. The popularity of concierge services stems from the fact that people are stressed out, overworked and need help dealing with life so they can spend their free time nurturing themselves and their families. As good workers become harder to find, businesses are looking for concierge services to offer as perks to keep valuable employees happy.

Working Mother Magazine recently put out a list of the top 100 companies to work for, and they all have seem to have one thing in common -- they are offering work/life benefits to their employees. Companies are finally focusing on the fact that people can not do it all and they need help. Consequently, companies are adding work life benefits such as day care centers, job sharing, dry cleaning pick-up/delivery, leave for new parents and many are even letting you work from home. Some companies are even adding on-site company chefs who will cook dinner for you to take home at the end of the day! Others are developing programs to help you care for your elderly parents.

And of course concierge services are being added as part of corporate benefits packages.

The work/life idea is taking off like the proverbial brush fire and is reaching almost every corner of the United States. Two years ago there were only a handful of concierge companies around the nation. Today, with the work/life revolution becoming more and more popular, there are probably over 1000, and more are popping up every day. In-house concierge departments are also popping up as are lobby concierges.

People are embracing concierge and errand services because they give individuals more time to spend both at his/her desk and with their families at night. It is the classic win-win situation In addition, real estate management companies are offering lobby concierge services to their tenants to add value to their properties and increase their marketability.

These "lobby" concierge concierge companies are placing concierge services in office buildings to provide personal and business services to tenants. The concierges offer a host of services that include picking up dry cleaning, managing catered business lunches, picking up theater tickets, ordering dinner and shopping for clothes. They become friendly faces that clients see on a daily basis that can help them manage their lives. Personal service, it seems, is the hallmark of the concierge business.

One question the media always seems to ask me when they call is where I think the concierge industry will be in a few years. Well, I can best answer that question through a little history ...

After I graduated from college in 1984, I found a job working as an administrative assistant to a meeting planner. After a few months I quickly found out that not only did I enjoy the work, but I had an aptitude for it. However, in those days there were no books or courses you could take to learn meeting planning. You just learned it from the bottom up while in the field. Not many people knew what a meeting planner was back then, and certainly no one was teaching the subject in college.

Today meetings are a billion dollar industry. Colleges are offering majors in meeting planning, seminars are being taught around the world, associations have been created for meeting planners, and hundreds of books have been written on the subject. The concierge industry is going to go the same way as the meeting industry, it just isn't going to take 15 years to do it. In fact, I predict it will only take about 5 years or less.

Soon, most companies around the nation will be offering concierge services as part of a benefits package. Apartment buildings and businesses will offer concierge services to tenants and businesses, and everyone will not only have access to a service near them, but they will be able to afford it.

Most of all, they will also be able to finally spell and pronounce the word concierge!

Chapter 1

What skills do I need to become a successful concierge?

You have to be the type of person who will labor until the work is done no matter what time it is. If you are the type of person who leaves work at exactly 5:00 p.m. no matter what, then may I suggest that you read this section very carefully before embarking on this new venture. The client always comes first, no matter what, and if that same client needs some work finished by a certain day then you need to be sure to finish it, on time.

Experience in sales, marketing, meeting/event planning, human resources and customer service are all great things to have, but are not essential. I know of an excellent concierge who was an engineer in his "past life", and his business is flourishing. In the beginning you will be everyone — the bookkeeper, secretary, receptionist, errand runner, meeting planner, webmaster, business owner, mail room clerk, administrative assistant, president and chief bottle washer. You are the classic Girl (or Boy) Friday who does everything for everyone.

There is no such thing as a time clock when you own your own business, just like there is no such thing as a paycheck. I jokingly complained for months that I was the classic case of "overworked and never paid", but if you can hold on, the payoff is big because eventually your concierge business will soar. In this business you can't wait for things to come to you, you have to go to them. You need to be able to talk to virtually anyone about anything. The type of person who can have a conversation with a post in the subway. You should be able to radiate enthusiasm when talking about your business, and you need to be able to work steadily day and night without complaint.

When you own your own business you have to be everything to everyone. If you have children at home then you not only have to balance everything in your new business but you also have to find time for the kids. I myself have a husband and two small children and balancing them makes me feel like a tightrope walker sometimes, but it is worth it.

The good news is that owning my own business allows me to set my own schedule and I can be there for my kids when they need me. It gives me the freedom to come and go as I please and work at my own pace. Further, since my office is in my home the commute is great! No more rushing home at 3:00 p.m. (breaking every speed record in the book, by the way) so I can make it to the school bus on time. I also always carry my cell phone with me so I can return telephone calls and speak with clients anytime day or night. This may appear to be intrusive, and at times it feels that way, but in my opinion it is essential in business that the client feels that their needs come first.

The downside to this? When there is a blizzard outside and

everyone else gets the day off because the roads are completely impassable, you are the only lucky one on the block who can actually get to work.

So, what type of person do you have to be? Outgoing, friendly, completely honest, open, talkative and enthusiastic. A real "go-getter" if you will. You need to be willing to work crazy hours doing seemingly crazy things, and you absolutely must follow through. You need to be able to wear 50 hats at once. You need to be able to not only find the impossible but do the impossible. You need to be able to talk on the phone, work on the computer, answer a question from one of your staffers and chew gum all at the same time. And, most critically, you need to be willing to sacrifice a steady paycheck for a while.

<u>Make sure</u> that you have enough money in your bank account to last you a minimum of 6 months, preferably a year, because in the beginning, all the money you take in from your business will have to go right back into the business. Economize as much as you can. Use coupons. Drive a cheaper car. Cut back on luxuries. Don't eat out, brown bag your lunch. There are perhaps hundreds of ways to cut back (and at least as many books out there to teach you how to do it). So, essentially, you need to be willing to be "poor" for a while. As an entrepreneur it can be overwhelming in the beginning unless you are prepared for it emotionally as well as financially. So ask yourself, are you prepared?

While this picture may seem bleak to those of you who have never owned your own business, it offers a realistic glimpse at the beginnings of a new venture. A few years ago when we were starting our first company, Meeting Planning Plus, my husband and I were both working the business and neither one of us was earning a regular paycheck. We were financially overburdened, and stressed to the max! Talk about having to cut back on things! It was a little touch and go there for a while but we learned from this mistake and he went out and worked a "real job" (that included health insurance) while I got the business going. Once the company could afford to pay his salary, he returned to working with me full time.

The lesson here of course is this. If you are married to your business partner, make sure that one of you has a steady income coming in as well as health and dental benefits. I also humbly suggest to all married partners out there that they each have their OWN desk, computer and telephone if they value their marriage. Trust me on this one because I am the voice of experience. At one point Ron and I were sharing a desk and computer in the basement of our house. It seemed to be the most cost-effective solution at the time because we could only afford to buy one of everything and sincerely thought that we were capable of sharing.

NOT!

We always needed to use the desk and computer at the same time, and we each thought that our own work was the most important (of course) and should take priority. So we starting fighting about it. It drove me crazy!! Soon, however, we found a solution to the problem. We had to separate. Separate our

work spaces that is. Once we moved apart, we no longer
quibbled about who needed the desk more. Today, my office is
up in the bonus room and his is in the den. We each have a
desk, computer, telephone and fax. We don't bicker any more
(at least about this issue) and the peace is back. So if you love
your spouse then let them go ... so to speak.

If you are single, as mentioned before, make it a point to have
at least 6 month's salary saved in a readily accessible bank
account before you begin. Either way, it is best to work out
most of the details that I will be outlining before you quit your
current job. Create the framework for your business at night,
on weekends, or even by taking a week long vacation to stay at
home and work. Once the details are all ironed out, then you
can quit your current job and start working on your new
business full time.

Ultimately, my advice all boils down to one old saying that my
mother used to say to me --- "do as I say and not as I do". Just
because I made all of these crazy mistakes certainly doesn't
mean that you have to.

Opportunity

"People think that at the top there isn't much room. They tend to think of it as an Everest. My message is that there is tons of room at the top."

Margaret Thatcher

Chapter 2
Business Basics

This chapter's purpose is to provide you with a brief overview on how to get your concierge service going. There are many excellent books available that have been written on the subject of starting your own business, so I really don't think it necessary to go into a huge amount of detail here. A list of suggested books and websites are listed at the end of each topic where appropriate (as well as at the end of this book). Please remember that these are all only <u>suggestions</u> on how to get your business going. They are all simply ideas that have worked for us.

Company Name and Logo

Let's start at the very beginning with your company name. Generally it is wise to choose a name that aptly describes the service that you intend to provide. As a result, words that describe what your service does (like "concierge" or "errand") should probably appear somewhere in your title. Does your area or state have a nickname that people use? In our case we used the word (and symbol) "triangle" because our area is nicknamed "the triangle".

The logo should start simply. Try using Microsoft Word's "WordArt" or other similar product to give you some ideas. They offer a bunch of different styles that you can use to create your logo. Shapes and symbols are also good to use. If one exists, look into using a symbol/shape that represents your city.

Legal Issues and Contracts

It would be extremely wise to consult a lawyer <u>before</u> starting
your company. He/she will be an excellent resource for you and
will assist you in getting incorporated. Be sure the lawyer you
choose has experience in business law. A good lawyer can offer
practical advice on how to get your business going, what
permits and licenses you need and they may even be able to
give you the name of a great accountant. It really pays to do
things right the first time around.

First and foremost <u>you need a contract</u>. The last thing you
need is a lawsuit. You should have a member/client contract to
protect you from liability issues as well as a simple service
vendor agreement stating that you are not responsible for the
vendor. Each member should fill out a membership application
and sign the contract. Ours is about a page and a half long and
is pretty straightforward. Sample contracts may be purchased
by going to our bookstore at www.triangleconcierge.com. You
can also find service agreements in the contract section of
www.entrepreneurmag.com.

We have one contract to cover three separate types of services:
individual, corporate and lobby concierge. It includes terms
and services, customer responsibilities, compensation and fees,
termination, relationship of the parties, warrantees and
disclaimers, indemnity by customer, limitation of liability and a
miscellaneous section. We have another contract that service

vendors are required to sign before we allow them onto our business referral service, and we have a third contract for meeting and event planning.

Remember though, that because the concierge industry is so young lawyers do not have any guides or samples to follow when creating a contract for you. So they will be forced to come up with something out of thin air, and they will charge you accordingly. Ours charged us $1,500. So, if you can find another contract for them to just read over (as opposed to creating) then your cost will lower substantially.

No matter whose contracts or agreements you choose to purchase, ***please make sure*** that you have your own lawyer go over it first because each state (and each country) has its own laws and guidelines. Remember, doing it right the first time will avoid any consequences that may pop up. In the long run this will save you a bunch of money.

If you plan on doing any of the meeting or event planning yourself then it is necessary for you to have a contract. This is VERY IMPORTANT! It should outline exactly what you have been hired to do in detail. It should have a basic indemnity clause, act of God clause, cancellation clause and liability clause. If your client were to cancel the event one-week before it is scheduled to occur, what do you do? The hotel will penalize you and you are out a lot of money for the hard work that you've done. Again, a good lawyer can draw a contract up for you if you don't want to use ours.

Meeting Professionals International has some wonderful books on this very subject that can be purchased on-line from their bookstore at www.mpiweb.org. Having the appropriate contracts is one of the **most important** parts of setting up this service (the other is insurance). You need someone who can watch your back in case someone sues you. Contracts and insurance will provide this.

If you don't go with a lawyer, call your city municipal building and ask them what the procedure is to incorporate. Also ask them about what permits and licenses you will need to have to start operating.

So my advice is this.... Before you start, find a good lawyer, a great accountant and some good insurance because it is more than worth the time and money. Doing it right the first time will save you from a great deal of unnecessary hassles

Accountant

It is also extremely wise to get a good accountant to do your taxes and offer you advice on how to get your books off the ground, how to set up your business and what resources you will need to purchase. Should you be an s-corp or a LLC or something else? Your accountant knows the tax laws in your particular area and has the necessary wisdom to advise you properly.

One resource we use is *QuickBooks*, recommended by our own accountant. It is a wonderful product that we use to keep our books, invoices and records. However, if you do not wish to purchase Quickbooks, you can use a spreadsheet program like Microsoft Excel.

Finally, there is a wonderful webpage where you can purchase all your spreadsheets and forms located at www.villagesoft.com/msprods/solution.htm.

Insurance

Everyone needs it and if you're using your spouse's insurance, great! If you're not, then you have to begin shopping around for it. You might also want to give it to your employees as a benefit (once you get employees that is). The following information is not meant to replace that offered by accredited insurance agencies. It is meant only to be used as a guideline.

Health Insurance

If you already have insurance because you are on your spouse's insurance plan, this will not apply to you. If you don't and you have to go on Cobra when you quit your job, then by all means keep it for as long as you can. However, once you hire employees (or the Cobra runs out) then you will have to get some health/life insurance. It is best to shop around for the best price. Go directly to the company's themselves to get the best pricing plan for your needs. You might also want to consider dental insurance, which we have found to be very valuable over the years.

Business Insurance

It is not a question of what you think your business is worth, but it is more accurately what you think the largest amount someone could sue you for is. It would be unrealistic to think this could never happen and it is better to be prepared. Business insurance is extremely valuable in the concierge business because of the high amount of liability. To cover yourself, you need business insurance because without it they can take your personal assets. A good insurance person will be able to guide you in this more thoroughly.

Unfortunately many of our clients are having a terrible time getting business insurance because not only is the industry only a decade old, but there is no category to put us in. Generally, I suggest to all my clients that they go to an independent insurance broker because they are more "flexible" and can search many companies instead of just one (try several independents).

I also suggest that you tell him/her that they should put you into the "limousine driver/taxi" category or the "cleaning house" category. Also, tell them that it is your company policy to never enter a home unless someone is there. The liability factor of this particular service is scaring a lot of companies away and this simple thought seems to make them feel much better. If you actually want to go into someone's home take it on a case by case basis and get them to sign a liability waiver that your lawyer can draw up. If they want you inside of their home that badly, they'll sign it. Bonding each employee will help this too. One could say that we are similar to a cleaning company in that we both go into people's homes when they are not there so why is there such a problem? The problem lies in the fact that insurance companies are seeing the additional services that a concierge provides ... like errand running in your car or recommending a service vendor (like a deck builder) for example, and other risk management type of tasks and are thinking "high liability". It is the liability that the insurance companies worry about.

More to the point, insurance companies don't know who we are and need education on it. They have no idea what a concierge is or does. You see, insurance is based on codes. This is how they gather their information and develop their risk management policies. Through the codes. Since the concierge business is new, they are unsure as to where to put us because there is no history or code for "concierges", and the history is how they set up their premiums. Insurance companies (like everyone else) want to make money, and unless there is a proven history of good risk management it is hard to convince them to give coverage.

Bonds

It is true that you should be able to trust your employees, but according to the U.S. Chamber of Commerce, the fact is that one-third of all employees admitted stealing from their employers during the previous year. Consequently, if you are hiring employees to run errands for you or do some "modified house sitting" (which I will explain in a later chapter) you will have to purchase **Employee Dishonesty Bonds** in addition to your business insurance. These Bonds will protect you from dishonest acts by your employees. It is wise to purchase one bond per employee so that you are fully protected from any theft or embezzlement that may occur.

Lastly, it would be advisable to have each employee sign a simple non-compete clause that your lawyer can draw up for you. You certainly don't want to train your competitors!

Chapter 3
Business Plan

Everyone who starts a new business should have a business plan. Not only will you need one if you plan on obtaining any sort of financing, but it will help organize your thoughts and focus your direction. When writing one you will focus and set your goals and you will identify the problems and pitfalls that you might face. Your business plan should not be long and cumbersome and should clearly outline what your business is, where you plan on going, and how you are going to get there.

There are some wonderful business plan software packages, great websites and numerous books available on the subject. We have listed several good ones in our reference section. Using one of these guides will help to set up your business and make long range plans. Your business plan should include the following topics:

Chapter I: **Executive Summary**
Introduction
Mission Statement
Unique Features
Marketing Objectives
Expected Accomplishments
Required Capital

Chapter II: **The Business**
                         Problem Statement
                         Description of the Business
                         Founder(s) of the Business
                         Management and Operations
                         Objectives

You will also need to include the financial information described in the pricing section of this book within your business plan. If you need help writing your business plan, a search on the web will prove useful. I found some wonderful companies who were very helpful. Some gave me descriptions of each topic and others gave actual samples. Although you can hire people to write a business plan for you, I would advise against it. There is enough information available for the entrepreneur to save the money for something else.

When I created our business plan I used the Smart Business Plan Software (which can be purchased in many stores and mail order companies that carry business software). It is a helpful step by step guide that easily helps you to create your own business plan. Another good one is Business Plan Pro. I suggest that you look at some of the sample plans on www.bplans.com to use as guides and then purchase Business Plan Software to help you write it, it is well worth the price.

There are several parts to a business plan that everyone should include. These sections can be clearly seen in the business plan example found at the end of this book. It provides clear examples of how each section could be written

for a concierge company. Please note that these are only
examples and are written to provide you with a simple guide
when creating your own plan.

Remember, the purpose of a business plan is to provide the
reader with a comprehensive synopsis of a business. Therefore
we are using the fictional name of "Sample Concierge" as the
company name. Please note that this paragraph is to be an
introduction to your business and should state exactly what
month and year the business started, who started it, where,
when business operations will begin and the type of service you
want to provide. Since it is the first one people will read, it
must therefore capture their interest. It is also the one
paragraph that everyone will read thoroughly.

Furthermore, if you are using this plan to obtain capital, then
you should state the amount of capital you need in the
"required capital" section of your plan. Clearly explain how you
will repay the money and the reason why you need the capital.
If you are seeking investors such as venture capitalists then it
is in this section where you should tell them what the return on
their investment will be and how long it will take them to get
it.

As previously stated, you will find a very simple concierge
business plan at the end of this book. Please remember, that
this plan in merely included as an example, and serves as
a guide for when you sit down to write your own. The numbers

are ficticious and only serve as an example of how a table might look. I find that it is always 100% easier to create something new when I have a sample to follow.

Chapter 4
Getting Started

Do <u>NOT</u> quit your job, go out and rent an office, buy or rent furniture and hire employees. THINK ABOUT IT FIRST! Ok, I'll admit it. I've made that mistake too. We actually did rent an office and purchase furniture with the thought that we would need the office for our future employees. Of course once everyone knew who we were and what we were doing then our phone would be ringing off the hook! Right?

Unfortunately it didn't happen that way but it was a nice dream while it lasted. After a while, it dawned on us that the little profit we were making was just going into paying for our monthly overhead. In fact, we were using both our personal savings and our profit to cover the office overhead which of course left us nothing left over to pay for groceries and other necessary items ... like the mortgage! So we closed our little office and moved the entire operation into our home. The lesson here? Work out of your house until you feel that you can afford an office because in the beginning, you definitely do not want the overhead (or the headaches!).

Instead, convert a small space in your home into an office. You will need a desk, a good computer with a color printer (preferable but not absolutely necessary) and a fax machine. It is best and the most cost effective to buy a fax/copier/telephone all in one. Also good to have is a filing cabinet and some office supplies on hand (things like pens, paper, post-it notes, paper clips, stapler, file folders, and the like). Buy a couple of stackable in-boxes because it will help you organize your desk. Organize the boxes into categories like "to be read later", "in", and "out", "file" and the like.

Organize file folders in your filing cabinet in the following categories:

- Accounts payable
- Accounts receivable
- Articles of incorporation
- Audio-visual
- Catalogs
- Computer
- Contracts
- Correspondence
- Entertainment
- Insurance
- Legal
- Local hotels
- Marketing
- Media
- Membership Affliations
- Music
- Out-of-state hotels and resort properties
- Paid bills

- Personnel
- Proposals
- Prospects
- Receipts (business)
- Restaurants
- Service Vendor Contracts and Applications
- Service Vendor Brochures and Information
- Speakers
- Transportation

Organizing your folders now will save time later and as you begin to research your service vendors and meeting/event locations. When a client calls you, you need to have the information at your fingertips so you can get them an answer as quickly as possible.

Finally, it's a good idea to put a second line into your house that you can use for your new business. The second line can double as your fax, modem, and telephone line. In most areas your local telephone company can fix you up with an automatic answering machine so that when your line is busy, the call will automatically be forwarded to your voice mail.

Letterhead and Business Cards

Do yourself a BIG favor and do not go out and buy expensive business cards and letterhead. In the beginning when you have the time, save your money and do it yourself on your computer. A good software product that we use is *Broderbund's Printshop Deluxe version 6.0*, although there are many good ones on the market. You could create letterhead in Microsoft Word and Adobe as well. These software programs include tools that will help you create some really nice business cards, letterhead and brochures for your new business at a reasonable cost. Buy some good 25-pound paper and some nice business card stock and be your own printer until it costs you more in lost time to do it yourself.

An ideal business card for an errand/concierge service is the type that folds in half. The outside is your business card with your contact information written clearly. When you open it up it is a micro-brochure with a quick list of some of the services you offer on the inside of it. On the back you could put your picture and a catchy phrase of some sort. (If you have no idea what I'm talking about perhaps this will help ... this type is like two business cards fused together.)

Brochure

When creating your first brochure, look around at what other people have done. Figure out what services you wish to provide and then list them in your brochure. Avoid being too wordy because most people are in a hurry and won't take the time to read a verbose brochure. They are looking for brief, concise overviews outlining the highlights. Save the detailed explanations for your "sales kit". Broderbund's software (mentioned above) includes a really nice wizard that will easily guide you through the brochure process step by step. We have found it to be extremely useful.

What you should include in your brochure:

1. An **Introduction** to your service explaining what a concierge is and does as well as what it can do for the individual or corporate entity.
2. A **list of services** that you provide.
3. A **Reference list** of reputable local businesses you can refer them to.
4. **Membership Information**
5. Your **company name**, **address**, **telephone** and **fax numbers, e-mail address** and **website** address.

Use nice bright colors, borders and graphics to make your brochure attractive and easy to read. Again, look around at other people's brochures to see what aspects appeal to you and implement them into your own brochure. When you are finally ready to get the piece printed shop around! Go to at least 3 printers and get the best price. Don't forget that if this printer does a good job for you then you can put them on your service and refer them out to dozens of people. This is a great incentive for them to not only give you a good price but to also do a good job so that you will refer them to your clients. Remember, a good marketing piece grabs attention, gives information and most of all causes a response of some kind.

In the brochure you should absolutely make it stand out. Get attention and make it as classy and special as possible. Write the text to be short and readable in a 10-12 font size (don't use script as its hard to read). Use bullet copy points to draw interest and make sure you tell them how the services will benefit the client. Sell it! Tell them! What problems will it solve? Don't use reverse copy (white words on black) or watermarks as this is also very hard to read. You should also end the brochure with a call to action. CAUSE a response! Use testimonial quotes as they are a very powerful sales tool. Lastly, NEVER mail it just once. Many believe it takes at least 4-5 mailings before someone will respond.

Sales Kit

First, go out and buy some pocket presentation folders. Then purchase some 1/2 page size labels to put your logo on. Voila! Personalized sales kit folders. Once you begin making the "big" money you can go out to a printer and get some really terrific sales presentation folders made up with your logo on it. For the moment, however, this is the most cost-effective method.

What you should include in your Sales Kit:

1. An introduction/welcome letter.
2. Detailed explanations of all the services you intend to provide.
3. Membership details.

4. Membership contract and application (if that is how you're setting up your service). If not you should include information on how to join your service.

5. A sheet listing your current rates (subject to change without notice)

6. Your business card.

7. Your company brochure.

8. Your company newsletter

9. Articles that people/magazines/newspapers have written about you.

10. A reference list of satisfied clients that can be added later once you get a few. Be sure to get your client's permission before you list their name in your kit.

Setting up your databases

You will need a good database like *Microsoft Access* to hold all the information about your clients. No matter what software you choose, you'll have to keep a database of your members/ clients outlining their likes, dislikes, and address. We use *Microsoft Access* because you can design your own database to suit your needs. Should you indeed opt to do the database yourself, then Microsoft sells a wonderful training CD that will teach you how to use Access. You can usually find the program in your local store next to Access.

No matter what database you decide to use, there is certain

information that you will need to know like:

- The clients name
- Company name
- Work address
- Home address
- Work phone
- Home phone
- E-mail address
- Spouse name
- Kids
- Interests
- Payment information
- Credit card/check payments
- and notes

As with all the other programs we have mentioned, however, you should shop around for the one that suits your specific needs. I just like Microsoft Access because it is so versatile. Each member/client should receive an ID card with your company name, address, phone number and e-mail address on one side and their company name and ID number on the other. You can save yourself some money and generate these cards from your computer using business card stock and the type of program you use for your brochures (such as Broderbund Presswriter for example).

The member/client database might include the following fields:

Customer ID	Birthdate Date
Member ID	Updated
Prefix	Client Status
First Name	Hobbies
Last Name	Health Issues
Nickname	Marital Status
Title	Spouse Name
Company	Spouse Interests
Address	Childrens Names
City/State/Zip	Acccount Balance
Home Phone	Payment Method
Work Phone	Credit Card Type
Email Address	Credit Card #
Fax Number	Expiration date
Date	Cardholder Name
Description of current tasks	Notes

You also might like to design a database for restaurant information. When a client calls and asks you to make a restaurant recommendation for them, you and your staff members need to get the information to the client as soon as possible. This database streamlines the operation so that the information can be at your fingertips as opposed to flipping through the pages of a lengthy restaurant guide.

This database might include the following fields:

- Restaurant ID
- Restaurant Name
- Address
- City
- State
- Zip Code
- Country
- Telephone Number
- Website Address
- Food Type
- Reservations Required?
- Rating
- Price Range
- Date last updated
- Notes

Lastly, you might want to create two more databases ... a service vendor database and a mailing list database for potential clients. Generally, a company has to see your direct mail piece approximately 8 times before they will pick up the telephone and dial your number. The database might include the typical name, address and telephone information that would normally go onto labels or in a personalized form letter.

Once all the databases have been set up you might want to consider networking your computers so that all your employees can have access to the information in the databases (of course one should probably have employees first!).

Lastly, if you decide that you do not have the time to do it yourself then Triangle Concierge sells some reasonably priced Concierge Software that has everything you need to get you started. It includes databases for client contact information, personal information, vendor database, restauarant database and pertinent financial information. Just log onto their website at www.triangleconcierge.com for all the details.

Getting Ahead

"To get it right, be born with luck or else make it. NEVER give up. Get the knack of getting people to help you and also pitch in yourself. A little money helps, but what really gets it right is to NEVER , I repeat, NEVER under any condition face the facts"

Ruth Gordon

Chapter 5
Website Creation Made Easy

When it comes to websites you have two choices. One, you do it yourself. Two, you pay someone to do it. At one point I considered hiring someone to do it for me until they quoted me their price (which I thought was ridiculously high) so I opted to do it myself with the help of a good friend. It will cost you very little money to do it yourself, just $70 to register the name with Internic. If I can teach myself how to do it, so can you! One of the benefits for being your own webmaster is that you can make changes quickly and easily from your own computer at the exact moment that you think of them. If you hire someone else to maintain your site for you then you will have to forward the changes/additions to him or her. Although it may take you some time to learn, it is well worth it in the end.

E-mail versus URL

For those who are not sure about the difference between e-mail and URL, here are their definitions.

1. **E-mail:** is a communication tool. Think of it as your telephone number. It is a fast and easy way to communicate with others.
2. **URL (Uniform Resource Locator):** Think of this as your address. It is a great place for people to find information

about both you and your company.

Internet Service Provider

First, before you do anything else you need to get access to the web. Choose a good Internet service provider (ISP) like Mindspring, BellSouth, Microsoft, or America Online. Make sure that whatever provider you choose has several local phone numbers available. There are a lot of companies out there but some are certainly better than others. A good company will offer you both Internet access, with at least one e-mail account and the software you need to get you started. Shop around, and find the one that best suits your needs.

Setting up your URL

Your website name can be your company name or the name of your product and generally will look like this: www.yourcompanyname.com. Once you choose a name, you must register the name with Internic who will hold it for you for 2 years for $70. In essence, you register with Internic to make sure that your name is available and not already being used by someone else. To register with them is really easy. Just go to www.register.com and follow the instructions.

Creating the page

Once you have chosen your Internet provider it is time to build your WebPage. The software that I use is Microsoft's Frontpage. It is extremely easy to use and makes very professional looking webpages. If, however, you don't have the funds to purchase this software, and prefer instead to use Microsoft Word then here's what to do. Click on "file" and then "new", then click on "web pages". If your software has the **webpage wizard** it will be listed right there, just click on it. If it doesn't just click on "what's new" and it will tell you how to get it from Microsoft as a free download (which is how I got it actually).

If you use another software product that you find better…great! I only listed Microsoft's products because it is what I use and makes for a good example.

Keep your page as simple as possible because people are generally in a hurry and don't want to spend a lot of time on any one page. Also, remember that you want your page to load quickly so try and not use too many fancy graphics or dark colors. People log onto your website for the information that it provides, not for the dancing cows. Keep it clear and easy to read. Bright colors and nice wallpaper all serve to make your page more attractive. Look around at other people's Websites to get some ideas for your own page.

Pay careful attention when you name your pages in Microsoft word. The first page of the site should be named *Index*. The rest can be named whatever you wish. All should be saved as an html documents. Be careful with the graphics because sometimes they don't load well and if there is a space in their name then it will cause problems. **No** spaces! (trust me on this one, I learned it the hard way).

If you have more than 1 page then you will have to create a *hyperlink* to each page. For those who don't know, a *hyperlink* is a way to travel from one page or site to another, it is an easy way to expand your website. Frontpage does the hyperlinks for you, Microsoft Word does not. For example, on my page (www.triangleconcierge.com) I have a list of contents at the left-hand side of the page listing all the topics. Each topic is *hyperlinked* to another page. Now, suppose you want to have a second page called "manual"? This is what you need to do if you are using Microsoft Word:

- First create the page using your Microsoft Word Web Wizard (an easy way to do this is to **copy** the index page and **paste** it into a blank web page using the wizard, then just change the words around).
- Type the word "manual" onto the index page somewhere, highlight it, and go to the **insert** menu and click on **hyperlink** located at the bottom of the list.
- Simply type in the name of the page (www.triangleconcierge.com/manual.htm) that you want to

link the index page to into the box labeled "link to file or
URL.

All people have to do now is simply click on the word "manual"
on your index page and they will automatically go to your
second page. However, as I stated above, if you use Microsoft
Frontpage then the software does the hyperlinks for you.

Finding a Web-Hosting company

Now you are ready for a web-hosting company who will host
your website. There are a lot of these companies out there so
shop around for the best price. A good way to look is to do a
search on "web hosting" and find the one that best suits your
needs (we use www.aismedia.com). Internet providers such as
Bellsouth and Mindspring are examples of web hosting
companies and you can expect to be charged anywhere from
$9.95 a month to hundreds of dollars to host your page, it just
depends on the needs and size that you require. BEWARE!
Know what you are buying! Also remember that you can
change hosting companies anytime you want to.

Web Publishing

Ok... now you've chosen your ISP, registered your site with
Internic, written your page, found a company to host your page
and you are set to go. Now it is time to move your page from
your own computer to the web. I use WS FTP Pro

(www.ipswitch.com) to do this and it is available to be purchased on the web. It is very simple to use and fast (simple is good for us self-taught people!). Make sure you request the instructions when you download. As with all of these issues, there are plenty of products available both on the Internet, and at your local software supply houses. Simply choose the one that appeals to you.

A very good friend of mine once told me that a webpage is actually a living and breathing thing and needs to be updated as often as possible to keep it new and fresh. Go to your page at least once a day just to make sure that it is still there and working properly. Once every few weeks add a new page, change something, and update some words...keep working on it. It is like decorating a house...you just never seem to finish it. Remember to add things like newsletters, updates, and new vendors to keep your page fresh.

Search Engines

Ok, you've created the page, found a provider, posted the page and everything works (click on everything just to make sure all your links work). Now you have to get people to actually go to the page and read it. There are a great many ways to do this, but for our purpose let's just keep it simple.

First, go to the site www. jimtools.com. You can register your website with the top 46 search engines for free! The site will also give you some great information about your meta tags. However, you should register with Yahoo yourself. To register, go to yahoo and find the category you wish to be listed under. Once you're on that page go to the bottom and click on "add a site". Then just follow the directions.

Remember that many search engines will only keep your page up for a certain period of time so you have to re-register your page with the search engines at least once a month. I do it twice a month. It won't take you more than an hour or so and is well worth it. Of course, a good webmaster will do this for you but he/she will also charge you a monthly fee.

I also go to a few of the top search engines myself (like AOL's Netfind) and simply click on "add a site" which is usually found at the bottom of the page. Some search engines can take up to 8 weeks to add your site so be patient.

For more information on search engines and how to get your site listed at the top, go to http://www.searchenginewatch.com.

It is also a good idea to advertise your website absolutely everywhere...on your answering machine, business cards, letterhead, company brochure, correspondence and even on the magnetic sign on your car! The signs allow you to advertise your company while you drive around the area. Two signs cost around $50.

Lastly, to protect yourself if you do decide to have a developer design your site, please remember to have them sign a non-compete/non-disclosure statement so they don't sell your information to the highest bidder. This happened to a friend of mine whose information got sold across state lines to various people.

Chapter 6
Setting up your Services

A Brief Overview

As good workers become increasingly hard to find in a hot U.S. economy, businesses are looking for new and effective ways to either attract or retain valuable employees. According to *Good Morning America* "absentee-ism has tripled at the workplace in the last year due to stress". Concierge Services alleviate some of that stress because it takes some of the day-to-day tasks off their shoulders. It creates some additional time for them to relax.

Companies around the nation will now be able to offer employees a host of services to help alleviate some of that stress — from picking up dry cleaning, running errands and managing catered business lunches to personal shopping, business referrals, ordering dinner and shopping for clothes. Instead of making 20 calls, the employee has to make only one.

There are many different ways to set up a concierge service. Some companies provide all of the following services, and others concentrate on only one. I think that it is important for you to understand how concierge companies in general set up their service so that you have a "sample" of sorts to follow when we begin to discuss your new service. Therefore, below is a brief overview of the various ways concierge companies set up their companies and the services that they provide.

Individual Concierge Services

This service is for everyone. It is the perfect gift for the holidays (or any other occasion) for anyone who is overworked, stressed out, and needs a little helping hand once in a while. Individual members are charged either a yearly membership fee or can choose to be charged on an "as they go" basis.

How to set it up - Clients may fax, e-mail or telephone their requests as often as they wish. Of course there are companies who limit the number of requests their clients can make on a per week basis. For example, some companies allow you 2-3 calls per week. Other companies allow unlimited requests.

Corporate Concierge

Corporate membership is designed for those companies who wish services via telephone, fax or e-mail. The cost can easily be made a part of either the company's employee benefit package or as a payroll deduction. Employees enjoy this service because it allows them to spend more time with their families, and their employers enjoy this service because it keeps them at their desks longer. They are more focused and can concentrate on the tasks at hand. A true win-win situation!

How to set it up - Once the contract is signed making you the company's exclusive concierge company, you should send each member/client a welcome packet of information about your company. This might included a list of all the services that you provide, rate information, and coupons for complimentary services. You actually want them to call as often as they can because the more they call, the more money you make in commissions from your service vendors. It is also a nice touch to mail your members/clients a monthly newsletter outlining new services, giving them coupons to use and providing them with other useful information. Doing this keeps your name in front of them as a reminder to use your service.

Each client should fill out a membership application when they use your services so you can provide them with the best service possible. Quite often you will take their information over the phone when they call you whether they are corporate or individual. Lobby concierges will get the information in person since the client is usually standing right in front of them.

You should try and provide personal service to everyone, so the more information you can get the more services you can provide to them that is geared towards their likes and dislikes and personal situation. Their specific requests are logged into the computer so you can remember them for the next time they call. And since personal service is the hallmark of the concierge service, your client's privacy is something that should be guaranteed. Assure your clients that you will not ever sell your clients name lists to outside vendors. In this type of business, it is critical that your clients trust you.

There are many ways to set this up. One way is to charge the company one discounted price per employee per year. Employees receive many services free-of-charge and some complimentary coupons. Errand services, meeting planning and personal shopping are generally extra.

Another way to set it up is to create a **concierge account** for each employee thereby eliminating the membership fee. The services and fees are then set up in a "restaurant menu" type of format. In other words, instead of going through the front door, try going through the back. Most corporations are getting hammered by increased insurance fees and have no additional money in their budgets for extra programs. Thus, a seemingly "free" service has a definite appeal.

The sales pitch here is to tell the potential client that they can now offer concierge services to each of their employees (and can make it a part of their corporate benefits package) FREE of charge! Yes...FREE of charge! Let me explain how....

You tell the potential client that there is no charge or membership fee for the service. Instead, you will create a concierge account for each employee in the company. You suggest that the employer put a minimum of $100 into each concierge account to get the employees started (this is how you receive the "seed" money that you need to provide the service). Not only are employees more apt to try the service this way, but the employer looks like the proverbial hero. "Here is this great service and we'll even give you some money to get you started with it"... sort of thing. Of course, it is completely up to the employer how much money they wish to put into each concierge account, $100 is merely a suggestion.

Corporations like to be in control of all situations. This idea is merely one way in which they can remain in control. They choose the amount of money that it will cost them as well as the services that they wish you to provide.

In your "sales pitch" you might tell the company that by making concierge services a part of their corporate benefit package their employee retention rate will increase. Further, as employees become less stressed out they will take less and less sick and personal days and their overall health and wellness will increase. It will also give them an edge on their competition. Finally, it will add another benefit to each employee's package at little (or no) cost to the employer.

The contact that you are seeking is with the company's **human resource department** because you want your services to become either a part of their corporate benefits package or a payroll deduction. To get your services in front of the Human Resources Director, however, you really do want to get the attention of the CEO, COO, President and the like. If they like the idea then the HR Director will be directed to look into it.

Once a contract is signed, the company should give you access to their employees by making you their "official" concierge. Then, they should send you a complete list of their employees and one contact person to call when you need to reach "the company". Your concierge company is then placed on their in-house telephone list (or a "concierge" button is added to their phones). The company might then send employees an in-house memo to let them know that your services are now part of their corporate benefits package. You should then send each employee a welcome letter and a list of your services and prices.

Each employee might also be given a membership card with an ID number on it so you can track him or her easily and add their requests to their page in your database. Finally, you might want to send the employees a monthly newsletter with various coupons as a way of keeping in front of them and reminding them to use your service.

Both a sample corporate proposal and a sales letter are included at the end of this chapter. I have always found that it is easier to create something new when you have a sample to follow. Remember, even if a company tells you that they prefer to do it in-house, then try and get some of the business outsourced to you such as the errand, meeting/ event planning and the like.

Lobby Concierge

A concierge desk is placed in the lobby of a building so that all the tenants (or employees) can benefit from your services. Not only will the tenants profit from having your services, but it will increase the value and marketability of the buildings, tenfold.

You can either charge the real estate Management Company a monthly rental fee, or you can offer the service to them for free and swallow the cost as you really just want access to all the individuals in the building.

The Lobby Concierge basic overhead is as follows:

1. Furniture rental including desk with drawers for files, lamp, and 3 chairs
2. Telephone installation
3. Fax, computer, printer, copier and various office supplies (pens, paper, rolodex, paper clips, folders)
4. Salary ($8 to $15 per hour) and benefits for the concierge

The bottom line, of course, is that you want it to be profitable. The contact here is your local real estate management companies. Call the area's top 10 and make them a pitch.

The concierge you hire to run the desk should be outgoing and friendly and should have experience in one of the following areas. Experience in sales and marketing, customer service, human resources and meeting planning are all great things to have. They need to be able to talk to anyone, anywhere, anytime. They need to be adept at finding the "hard to find" and solving the most difficult problem. They need to be able to keep their cool when confronted with an angry client. They need to be always smiling, a friendly face that people see everyday who can help them solve their scheduling problems. Remember that the concierge is going to have to be "on" all day.

In other words, they are representing you and will be in front of the public all day long so they must not only look neat and clean but must act accordingly. They should not be allowed to eat their lunch at the desk and they must all dress in business attire. Punctuality is a must.

Each concierge should personally introduce themselves and your service to each tenant in the building. They should develop an ongoing relationship with the tenants so that they can provide them with personalized service. Give out coupons to restaurants and other services as a way of drawing people to the desk. A detailed file should be kept on each person who uses the service because you want to track your customers. In other words, you want to learn about their needs, wants and requirements so that you can provide the services that they frequently use. Furthermore, you should encourage the concierge to quickly learn everyone by name so that they can receive a personal greeting whenever possible. Each concierge is given a salary and commissions based on each sale they make as an incentive to sell as many services as possible. The more money they make the more money you make. Simple. In addition, bonuses can be incentive driven.

Real estate management companies often tell the public that the needs of their tenants come first. By putting a concierge desk into the lobby of their building, they are actually proving it. They are also increasing the value and marketability of each building. As the need for office space grows, and more and more people go into business for themselves with the entrepreneurial dream, more incentives will be needed to drive them to your client's office buildings. Concierge services is that incentive.

Other Services

Other services are often provided as well. Several companies I know of specialize in errand and personal shopping services. Another company specializes in tickets, dinner reservations and finding the "hard to find" items. Yet another company specializes in the senior citizen market and delivers groceries and runs errands. Here are a few ideas:

Errand Service/Personal Shopping: You can set up an errand service and do your client's errands for them. Errands like running to the post office, picking up dry cleaning, going to the grocery store, hardware store, pet services, senior care, modified house sitting or picking up a gift at the mall. Anything goes here and it can be very lucrative. Figure that you can run at least 3-5 errands per hour, depending on what they are and their proximity to each other. You pay someone $8-15 per hour to run the errands for you (the rates really depends on the location) and you charge the client anywhere from $15-30 per hour (or you charge per errand) to run the errand. You can offer several "free" errand hours as an incentive to try the service. The client gets their errands done and the company makes a nice profit. This may not seem like a lot of money, but it adds up quickly. The trick is getting your clients to try the service.

Business Referral Service: This is a wonderful service that you can offer your clients. Once you have done the legwork, there is no additional cost involved and you can offer it for free. Some other concierge services charge the vendor a yearly fee to participate in the service. For others, vendors give a 10-15% commission on any business that results in a sale and the client gets the referral they need. Everyone needs a painter, electrician, plumber, insurance agent, or realtor from time to time, but you can't always be sure if you're getting the best when you randomly pick someone out of the yellow pages. You should personally interview each business, call their references and have them sign a contract thus ensuring a quality contact for your clients. Of course, if they don't comply with your agreement then you might wish to drop them immediately and replace them with a competitor. You are offering first class service to your clients, and if your vendors

don't also provide first class service, then they should be
replaced with someone who can.

Senior Assistance/Sick Care: There are so many senior
citizens out there who are not quite ready for a home, but yet
still need some assistance. They need someone to buy their
groceries and stock their refridgerator, pick up their
prescriptions, walk/feed their dog or cat, tidy up the house and
the like. Most of the time their adult children help out.
Children with families of their own to take care of! In comes
the concierge to the rescue. All of these "to do's" can be done by
a reputable concierge who can even call the adult child and tell
them "I'm here and your mom is fine". How to market this?
Not to the seniors because most do not have a dime to spare.
Market instead to the adult children who need an extra helping
hand in balancing their complicated lives.

On the following pages you will find a sample business proposal
that I used to send out to potential clients. I have included it
for you to use as a guide when creating your own proposals.

Sample Business Proposal

(should be printed on letterhead)

To: Toni Smith
        ABC Company

From: Katharine C. Giovanni
        President

Date: Insert current date

Re: <u>Concierge Services Proposal</u>

As promised, below please find our proposal for concierge services. If this proposal meets with your approval, then please call me and we'll set up an appointment for me to come see you so that we can set up the logistics and sign the agreement. If you have any further questions, please don't hesitate to call me at 555-555-5555.

The Problem:

· Stressed employees causing illness resulting in sick and personal days
· Loss of productivity
· Distracted Employees — long hours at work causes them to not be able to do the stuff they need to do to run their households.
· Employee Retention

Proposal, page 2

What we can do for your employees:

- Errands such as banking, video return, run to the post office, dry cleaning pick up and delivery, return library books, grocery shopping, pick up prescriptions, personal shopping, pick up newspapers/mail and water plants when you're on vacation, and give employees a helping hand when they are sick and can't go out.
- We can search for tickets for shows, sporting events and the like.
- We can coordinate travel and vacation plans, help you plan your wedding, event or party and can order and deliver all your flowers and gifts!
- Our business referral service can find your employees an honest and reliable landscaper, carpet cleaner, personal chef, financial advisor, realtor ... whatever they need.
- We can take care of all your VIP's needs. We'll meet them at the airport, find them a hotel, make restaurant reservations, give them an area tour of the triangle and even send fresh flowers and fruit to their room!
- We can help your employees when they're sick by picking up medicine, food and the like.
- We can plan their parties, birthday/anniversaries, holiday events and family reunions!

What can we do for ABC Company?

· By making concierge services a part of your corporate benefit package you will increase your employee retention rate.

· As employees become less stressed out they will take less and less sick and personal days and their overall health and wellness will increase.

· Offering concierge services will give you an edge on your competition when you are competing for top-notch employees.

· It will also add another benefit to each employee's package at **no cost** to the employer.

Logistics *(to be explained only after you have a signed agreement with your client)*

· You give us access to your employees by making us your "official" concierge.

· You then send us a complete list of your employees and one contact person to call when we need to reach "the company".

· You place us on your in-house telephone list (or add a "concierge" button to their phones)

· You send employees an in-house memo to let them know that our services are now part of their corporate benefits package.

· We will then send them a welcome letter and a brochure

listing our services and prices.
- Employees who use our service will be asked to open a concierge account with us. This can be done either by a credit card that we will debit or a reasonable cash deposit.
- Employees will be billed on a monthly basis. Errands and personal shopping require a minimum of 24 hours notice so that we can provide the best possible service. We will do our very best to provide same day service requests

How do we implement this?

- All you need to do is sign a simple agreement to make us your exclusive concierge company.
- Send each of your employees an announcement telling them that we are your official concierge company.
- Send us a list of your employees so that we can prepare personal membership packages for each of them. The membership kits will go out to your employees after you make the announcement.
- Lastly, in order to make this successful, we suggest that for those employees that wish to utilize the service, ABC Company puts a nominal contribution into their concierge accounts to get them going.

Lastly,I have attached our list of services and rates for your convenience.

If you have any more questions, please do not hesitate to call me at 555-555-5555. Thank you, I'm looking forward to hearing from you soon.

Sincerely,

Your Name
Your Concierge

Corporate Services and Fees

Membership Fee: Waived

Errand Service: $ per errand/hour (a detailed list of errand prices will be sent to each member)

Basic Member Services

· Dry cleaning delivery and pick up, grocery shopping, prescription pick-up/delivery, returning videos and library books, plus anything else you need us to do. Why not let us buy that special gift for you?
· Why not let us watch your house while you're on vacation by picking up the mail and newspaper and checking on the house. Call us while you're away and we'll tell you what's in your mail!
· During the holiday season let us mail out your holiday cards. We can send out the invitations and make those phone calls to arrange for your next party!
· Sick? Can't go outside? Need dinner delivered? Quart of milk? We can help!

The following complimentary services are included with each membership:

· Search for tickets to concerts and special events

- Travel and vacation assistance
- Business Referral Service
- Restaurant Recommendations and Reservations

Extended Services:

We also can plan all of your meetings and events. Our 15 years experience combined with the many relationships we have developed with area vendors and hotels makes us able to help you with all your event needs!

Events such as weddings, Bar Mitzvah's, cocktail parties, birthday/anniversary celebrations, holiday parties, picnics, family festivals and much more. We also plan meetings, seminars, conventions and expos.

This is a fee-based service. Please call us if you are interested and we'll be happy to quote you a rate!

List of Services and Fees

Grocery Shopping: Email, telephone or fax your grocery list to us and we'll purchase them for you and bring them right to your door! **Cost:** % of the total bill prior to coupons. $20 minimum.

Personal Shopping: General errands such as prescription pick-up/delivery, dry cleaning pick-up/delivery, video rentals, purchase a gift, return a gift, run to the bank, whatever you need, just ask! **Cost:** 3 errand special for $, within a 5-mile radius of the drop off point. Otherwise, we charge $ per hour depending on what you want done and where you want us to go. Call us for a quote.

Desktop Publishing: Basic typing as well as newsletters, brochures, and manuscripts whatever you need! **Cost:** $ per typed page. Please call for a quote.

Research and Information Services: We'll search the Internet and our list of contacts for whatever you're looking for! **Cost:** $ per 15 minutes. 15 minute minimum.

Modified House Sitting: While you're away why not let us bring in the mail and newspapers and generally check on your house? You can even call us and we'll tell you what's in your mail! **Cost:** $ first visit. $ each additional visit.

Property Inventory Video Service: We can take a video of the entire contents of your home! **Cost:** $ for 2 hours. Includes 2 videotapes.

88

Holiday Help: We can be that extra hand you've been wanting! We can wrap gifts, address and mail out holiday cards and invitations...whatever you need! **Cost:** $ per hour.

Senior Visits, Out-Patient Visits, Sick Assistance: If you have an elderly parent or friend, an individual who is ill or someone who has just been released from the hospital then we can help! We can provide them with non-medical help. Services include buying/delivery their groceries, prescriptions and running general errands. Making sure their pets are fed and walked. Helping them around the house with LIGHT chores, making phone calls for them and the like. **Cost:** $ per 30 minutes. Call us for a quote!

Correspondence Thank you notes, invitations, holiday cards, etc. **Cost:** $ per note or card

Party/Wedding Planning: You don't need to hire a wedding or party planner to take control of your wedding...you just need a little help from us! We can help you with your wedding, birthday, anniversary, holiday parties, family reunions and more!   We'll help you find the reception/event site, select a great caterer, entertainment, florist, photographer, games, gifts and more! We'll address and mail out the invitations, and can even write your thank you notes!

Proposal, page 10

Save time and money by calling us! **Cost:** Customized. Please call for a quote

Meeting and Event Planning: We are a full service meeting planners who can help you with your seminars, expos, conferences, and board meetings. Assistance with registration, logistics, travel, contract negotiations and the like. **Cost:** Customized. Please call for a quote

Services must be requested 24 hours in advance, but we will do our best to provide you our services if an emergency arises. Prices do not include the cost of the actual services, for example, the cost of the groceries, dry cleaning, movie rentals and the like. Prices are subject to change without notice.

Logistics

This service is a pre-paid service. We accept Visa, Mastercard and American Express. Members are requested to open a concierge account and retain a minimum balance of $100 in the account. The account will be used to pay for all services and fees. The frequency of use directly relates to how much you will be asked to keep in the account. However, if a client wishes to pay with their personal check, then the driver will pick up the check prior to running the errand.

If you wish to pay via your concierge account, then the driver will pay for the service in cash that is deducted from your account. If you wish to pay via credit/debit card then we will be happy to keep your credit card number on file and will charge your account whenever you authorize us to. ABC Concierge Company will never charge your account without your verbal permission first.

Office Hours: Office hours are from 9:00 a.m. to 8:00 p.m Monday through Friday. On Saturday we are open by appointment only. We will accommodate clients for emergency errands and after hours whenever possible. Requests for service can be made via <<*insert your company name, address, telephone number, fax, web address, email address, etc.*>>

Chapter 7
Fee Setting

Figuring out how much to charge is probably the most difficult part of starting up any business. It is especially hard in this business because the industry is so young and as a result there are no real guidelines to follow. The US Anti-Trust Act tells me that I cannot tell you what to charge, but I can certainly help you figure it out. Every market is different so fees are set according to a number of factors ... region, overhead and who you are marketing to.

Region - Since the cost of living (or the average salary of the area) varies from region to region, so do the fees. The fee I might charge someone living in New York City or Los Angeles, for example, will be different from the fee I might charge someone living in North Carolina or Utah.

Who are you marketing to? What are people willing to pay for your services in your area? Are you going after blue-collar workers or white collar, the city or the suburbs, upper or middle class? The price I would charge a middle class worker who earns $20-60,000 per year, for example, would be very different from the price I might charge an affluent type person who earns over $100,000 per year.

Overhead

It is helpful to establish four things before you set your fees so that you know where you need to be financially and where you would like to go in the future. (You will also need all of these numbers for your business plan).

1. Your daily labor rate
2. Overhead
3. Percentage you are going to spend towards marketing
4. Profit

Some firms break down their fees as follows:

1. Labor   30 to 40%
2. Overhead   20 to 30%
3. Marketing   20 to 30%
4. Profit   10 to 20%

Establishing your Daily Labor Rate

First you need to decide on the yearly amount that you are worth. For example, suppose you decide that you are worth $40,000 per year....

$40,000 per year
Divided by 261 work days
Total would be $153.26
Your daily labor rate in this case would be $153.26 (not including overhead)

Establishing Overhead

Overhead includes your fixed expenses that include: office rent, salary, office furniture, supplies, telephone bill, company credit cards, accountant fees, and marketing. Of course as your business expands so will your overhead. The trick is to keep it manageable! The following is a partial list of what your overhead might be:

· Office Rent
· Telephone
· Office Supplies
· Rental of office Furniture
· Postage
· Insurance
· Accountant Fees
· Legal Fees
· Printing
· Photocopying
· Personnel salary and benefits
· Dues and magazine subscriptions
· Memberships
· Marketing
· Business Licenses and taxes

Let me elaborate on a few items on the list... ·

Office Rent: Don't go out and rent an office until you have regular clients. Work out of your home until you get some clients and employees and need the additional space. Shop around for the best price and only rent what you need. A simple two or three room office should suffice in the beginning.

Telephone, Office Supplies, Rental of Office Furniture, Postage: Everyone knows it is always best to shop around for the best price and here is no different. From office supplies to telephone...shop around. Spend wisely, and save your receipts. If you need furniture look in the newspaper for companies who are selling theirs as you might be able to pick up some great stuff for low prices.

My grandmother had a saying that I carry around and use to this very day..."If you have good taste, you don't need a lot of money", and she was right. You can find some very tasteful furniture at bargain prices by going through the newspaper and second-hand shops (we did and I'll venture a wager that you would never know if you came to my office). You should also consider renting your furniture since sometimes rental companies have some great packages!

Insurance, Accountant Fees, Legal Fees: I can't stress this enough...do it right the first time. Call your insurance agent, lawyer and accountant BEFORE you open for business and consult with them on what you need to do. Show them the sample contracts, talk about your business plan and buy some insurance...it is more than worth it!

Printing, Photocopying: It is not necessary to rent an expensive copy machine in the beginning, just go out and buy a copier/fax/telephone all in one machine. It is more than worth it and will do the small jobs for you. The large jobs can be done outside the office at stores like Staples, Office Max, Office Depot or a commercial printer. As always, shop around for the best price. The good news here is that you might be able to get these people to become a "service vendor" and in which case you will earn a commission for each job you bring them. Once you get your business up and running you can rent a really good copier and do some of the smaller printing jobs yourself. Then, instead of paying a printer the per copy charge you can keep it for yourself. A lot of companies do this and it can be quite lucrative.

Personnel salary and benefits: If you have a staff, you will have to give them benefits (like medical and dental insurance). There are many options available in today's competitive market. Make sure you also give an employee handbook to each staff member that clearly states your policies. You can find an example of one at the end of this book.

Break Even Point - You reach your breakeven point when your expenses (including the money you invested into the business and/or loans) match your revenue. In other words, take all your expenses and overhead including all salaries, benefits and office/operation expenses, and match it with the revenue that is generated by the company. You are considered a profitable company once you have reached your breakeven point and you get out of the red. Also, you should keep excellent records for all expenses that your business generates. These include all office expenses, travel, entertainment, marketing materials and the like. If you spent it on your business to get business then it is an expense.

You also might be considering paying yourself a salary (or any partners that you might have). Whether or not this is a good idea really depends on how you would like to structure your company and the amount of revenue that you are generating. Also it would depend on the type of company you create (such as corporation, partnership, etc) and the best tax advantages to each, which you should of course discuss with your lawyer and accountant.

It might take a year or it might take a few years to show a profit. Revenue is the key to your growth and success! Continue to grow your revenue and find ways to cut expenses without hurting your business and slowing its growth is the key to profitability.

So our advice is this ... grow your business while keeping your expenses down. Try and not spend your money on unnecessary things (like expensive advertising, for example, or expensive letterhead and business cards). Make careful investments into your business as your company grows.

Fees - How much do I charge?

Fee setting is actually one of the elements of marketing your
service because it tells people that you are going to give them
quality services for their money. A low fee may bring you
clients initially but it might not be enough to sustain your
business. You can also set a "rack rate" type of fee so that
members can obtain a nice discount. A rack rate being the
highest rate that you would charge for a particular service.
Hotel's will offer their sleeping room rack rates to people who
walk in off the street. You can obtain a discount for the
sleeping room if you have a AAA card or a meeting planner has
negotiated a special rate for you. The same can be said for
your concierge services. Remember folks, you can always come
down from an advertised price, not up.

You might even want to consider conducting some market
research in your area to find out what people might consider
paying for a service like yours. Give them a range of choices
and see what they say! Call family, friends, and acquaintances
and just ask. The information you get back will be invaluable.

If you do decide to charge a yearly membership fee, it generally
does <u>NOT</u> include other services like meeting/event planning,
errand services, or personal shopping. Many concierge
companies will give their clients a few hours of complimentary

errand/personal shopping hours along with the membership, as well as a myriad of other "free" services. Other companies will limit how many times your client can call in per week. Many other companies do not limit the amount of times a client can call because the company generally gets a commission or a fee every time they do. Let me tell you what the market generally bears.

If you are providing multiple services to clients, then you may wish to have a membership fee. Concierge Services, on the whole, generally charge a yearly membership fee plus fees for other services. I have seen membership fee's range from $75 to $750 to $1,800 (or more) per year depending on their location. In other words, companies located in New York City and Los Angeles would charge on the "high" end, and other companies in places like Iowa, for example, would charge on the low-medium end. On top of the membership fee, companies charge the client (usually on an hourly basis) for many other services such as meeting and event planning, errand running, personal shopping and researching for a product or a service. Hourly rates also vary depending on the type and location of the service.

Some other companies offer free membership and allow their clients to "pay as they go" for services. These companies also sell various products to their clients. A detailed breakdown of all the services along with their costs is usually quoted to the client. For example, the quote would include rates for errand

and personal shopping service, meeting/event planning, special date reminder service.

For errands, I have seen charges ranging from $15 to $30 per hour. It really depends on the location and the logistics. Meeting and event planning hourly rates range from $50-200 per hour. Things like personal shopping and doing errands like waiting for the cable repairman are all charged hourly.

If you are setting up a Lobby Concierge business then I would suggest costing out exactly what the monthly overhead will be. Overhead such as salary for the person manning the desk, a desk or kiosk, several chairs, telephone, computer, and supplies (of course if the client supplies their own desk and chairs, the cost goes down). Add a small profit onto the number. Remember, you are not looking to make a huge profit on the real estate management companies, you just want to break even and cover your costs. In fact, what you actually want is access to all the employees in the building so they can use your service. As your tenants use your new service and take advantage of your wonderful vendors, your revenue will substantially increase. Not only do you obtain revenue from the errand service charges, but each service vendor will pay you a commission.

The profit here is in the commissions and errand services. The more dry cleaning you take to your official dry cleaner (many cleaners will give you a commission on the cleaning that you bring to him), the more errands you run, and the more business referrals that you give out ergo the more money you make. It is for this reason that you should consider offering your lobby concierge's a salary and commission based on the number of sales they do. It is a basic sales strategy, the more revenue generated by the on-site concierge, the larger his/her income will be. Therefore, incentives (such as bonuses) are a wonderful way to get them to increase their sales.

How is the Client going to pay for the services?

Good question. I suggest that you make your service a pre-paid one. By creating the concierge account, you are creating a pre-paid service. Clients know right from the start that everything must be paid for in advance with either their credit card, personal check, or the money currently in their concierge account.

What if you go out and purchase $75 worth of groceries for a client? When your errand driver gets to the house, the spouse answers the door and refuses delivery. All of sudden you're stuck with $75 worth of groceries! A pre-paid service solves this problem from the outset.

At the back of this book you will find some sample forms that many of our clients have found useful. Of course, you might want to rename the forms to suit your particular needs.

Chapter 8
Logistics

(Or what to do when the call comes in)

Mrs. Smith is on the telephone and would like you to book her vacation, find a hotel room, buy and stock her refrigerator with groceries and walk the dog while she's away. Ok, fine. Now how are you going to fill this request? What are the exact steps you are going to follow? In what order?

These questions all need to be answered, in full, so that you can provide Mrs. Smith the best service possible. By writing a logistic script, not only will you know exactly how to fill this order, but your employees will know it too. Training new employees and temporary employees will be a snap because all they need to do is learn the steps from the script! Even if you are a one-man show right now and have no employees, the scripts will still be beneficial to you because you will logistically know how you are going to fill each request. In essense, it will flush out all the bugs from your system before you open up your doors!

Here are some sample scripts that I wrote a few years ago. They are very detailed and include many things (like an Ops Manager) that you might not need right now so take them with a grain of salt, so to speak. Please remember that they are simply samples and are only included to show you how detailed your own scripts can be. Your own script can be as detailed or as simple as you wish.

Sample Scripts

Errand Script

1. Telephone call comes in
2. The errand form is completely filled out and the client information taken. What is needed, where, when and how will you pay.
3. Client is looked up in the database and their status is checked. Also checked is the status of their concierge account.
4. The call ends.
5. A copy is made of the form. Original (yellow) given to administrative/accounting and the copy (white) is given to operations (ops)
6. If order is to be done on the same day it is immediately taken to ops and handed to the manager.
7. If order is to be done on the next business day, then order is to be put in the ops box.
8. Administrative/accounting enters information into the computer and files the form in the pending file.
9. Ops receives the order and logs it onto their dispatch sheet.
10. They then assign the job to a driver and log the information onto the drivers trip sheet. Errand order form is also given to driver and attached to form.
11. If the errand is needed on the same day, ops will call the

driver on their cellphone. Driver then will pull over to the side of the road and will add the pertinent information to their trip sheet.

12. Ops will put the driver's trip sheet and errand forms into a manila envelope, which the driver picks up when they begin their shift. Driver also picks up enough cash to cover all the errands from accounting. Driver signs out money from accounting.

13. Driver does the errands

14. Driver returns and gives their envelope to ops. Any leftover money is given to accounting

15. Night ops manager will cross reference all the daily orders to make sure all the orders that had to be done were done. Receipts are matched with expenditures.

16. A copy of the driver log is made and put into the driver's file. The original drivers log, errand order form, receipts are all signed off and then given to accounting.

17. Accounting logs information into the computer. Updates concierge account, and generates any necessary invoices to either client or service vendors used.

18. White and yellow errand order sheet, driver log and other forms are all stapled together and the date and name of individual who completed the job(s) are written on the top. Forms are then filed under the client's name.

19. In-house errands/jobs such as meeting/event planning, word processing, information search and the like are entered onto the office board.

Signing up new member script

1. Telephone call comes in
2. A new member application is filled out
3. Pre-payment information is taken
4. If errands needed, go to errand script
5. If no errands needed then call ends.
6. Application information is entered into computer database
7. Application is filed under new member's name
8. Send new member a confirmation packet

Business Referral Script

1. Telephone call comes in
2. Client is looked up in database to find out if customer is active or not.
3. Client requests a business referral
4. Staff member puts client on hold and goes and gets the Rolodex.
5. Staff member looks up the business referral in the Rolodex and gives information to the client.
   If client wants more choices, then go to number 9
6. Call ends.
7. Staff member then calls the business that was referred and gives them the client name and telephone number.
8. Call ends.
9. If client wants more choices then client's telephone number is taken and client is told that we will research it and will

get back to them within the hour.

10. Staff member ends the call and logs onto Citysearch in the computer

11. Staff member researches the information using the computer and the yellow pages

12. Staff member then calls the client back with the appropriate information

13. The call ends

14. Information is logged into client's file in the computer.

15. Accounting is notified that a referral has been given.

16. In 3 days, staff member who took the call makes a follow-up call to the client to find out how the referral was and if they were treated appropriately, etc...

17. At the end of the month, a statement is sent to each vendor that outlines the referral number, name of customer. Vendor is to fill in the amount of job and the commission "blanks". Vendor sends back the appropriate amount to Triangle Concierge

Restaurant Reservation/Recommendation Script

1. Telephone call comes in

2. Client is looked up in database to find out if customer is active or not.

3. Client requests a restaurant recommendation for the following night

4. Staff member puts client on hold and goes into our restaurant database.

5. Staff member ask client what type of restaurant/food they wish and what city/location they wish to go.

6. Client answers

7. Staff member looks up the appropriate restaurant and gives information to the client. If client wants more choices then client's telephone number is taken and client is told that we will research it and will get back to them within the hour.

8. Staff member ends the call

9. Staff member researches the information

10. Staff member then calls the client back with the appropriate information

11. Staff asks client if they wish us to make a reservation for them.

12. If no, restaurant telephone number and information is given to client and the call ends.

13. If yes, what day and time would they like?

14. Information taken, and the call ends

15. Staff member immediately calls the restaurant and makes the reservation for client.

16. Information is logged into client's file in the computer.

Dry Cleaning Script

1. Telephone call comes in

2. Client is looked up in database to find out if customer is active or not. Concierge account status is looked up: how are charges to be processed - cash customer or credit customer?

3. Errand order form completed.
4. Call ends by confirming order to customer. Order is assigned an order number and the number is given to customer.
5. Call ends
6. A copy is made of the form. Original (yellow) given to administrative/accounting and the copy (white) is given to operations (ops) for routing.
7. Administrative/accounting enters information into the computer and files the form in the pending file.
8. Accounting puts a hold onto the customer's concierge account and then puts form into pending file for completion.
9. Ops receives the order and logs it onto their dispatch sheet.
10. They then assign the job to a driver and log the information onto the drivers dry cleaning trip sheet. The Errand order form is also given to driver and attached to form.
11. If the errand is needed on the same day, ops will call the driver on their cellphone. Driver then will pull over to the side of the road and will add the pertinent information to their trip sheet.
12. Ops will put the driver's trip sheet and errand forms into a manila envelope that the driver picks up when they begin their shift. Driver also picks up enough cash to cover all the errands from accounting.
13. Driver does the errand by going to client's home and picking up their dry cleaning. Then driver goes to nearest Medlin Davis and drops off the cleaning under the client's name. The date the cleaning is to be ready is noted on the driver's

Dry Cleaning Sheet.

14. Driver goes onto the next errand or goes back to OPS and gives their envelope to ops. Any leftover money is given to accounting

15. Night ops manager will cross reference all the daily orders to make sure all the orders that had to be done were done. Receipts are matched with expenditures.

16. Night ops manager will note what day the cleaning is to be ready and logs it onto the appropriate daily dispatch sheet.

17. A copy of the driver log is made and put into the driver's file. The original drivers log, errand order form, receipts are all signed off and then given to accounting.

18. On the appropriate day the cleaning is to be ready, OPS assigns a driver to go pick up the cleaning.

19. Driver picks up cleaning, logs the pertinent information onto their form and delivers cleaning to client's home.

20. Driver moves onto another errand. Once driver drops of his/her logs, Accounting logs information into the computer. Updates concierge account, and generates any necessary invoices to either client or service vendors used.

21. White and yellow errand order sheet, driver log and other forms are all stapled together and the date and name of individual who completed the job(s) are written on the top. Forms are then filed under the client's name.

Modified House Sitting Script

1. Telephone call comes in

2. Client is looked up in database to find out if customer is active or not. Concierge account status is looked up: how are charges to be processed - cash customer or credit customer?

3. Errand order form completed.

4. Call ends by confirming order to customer. Order is assigned an order number and the number is given to customer.

5. Call ends

6. A copy is made of the form. Original (yellow) given to administrative/accounting and the copy (white) is given to operations (ops) for routing.

7. Administrative/accounting enters information into the computer and files the form in the pending file.

8. Accounting puts a hold onto the customer's concierge account and then puts form into pending file for completion.

9. Ops receives the order and logs it onto the appropriate daily dispatch sheet.

10. On the appropriate day, they assign the job to a driver and log the information onto the drivers trip sheet. The Errand order form is also given to driver and attached to form.

11. If the errand is needed on the same day, ops will call the driver on their cellphone. Driver then will pull over to the side of the road and will add the pertinent information to their trip sheet.

12. Ops will put the driver's trip sheet and errand forms into a manila envelope that the driver picks up when they begin their shift. Driver also picks up enough cash to cover all the

errands from accounting.

13. Driver does the errand by going to clients home and picking up their mail and checking around the house.

14. Driver goes onto the next errand or goes back to OPS and gives their envelope to ops. Any leftover money is given to accounting. Client's mail is given to OPS.

15. Night ops manager will cross reference all the daily orders to make sure all the orders that had to be done were done. Receipts are matched with expenditures.

16. Night ops manager will note if another visit to the home is necessary and logs it onto the appropriate daily dispatch sheet if necessary.

17. A copy of the driver log is made and put into the driver's file. The original drivers log, errand order form, receipts are all signed off and then given to accounting.

18. On the appropriate day, driver visits the home again.

19. Number 35 and 36 are repeated.

20. Driver moves onto another errand.

21. Once driver drops of his/her logs, Accounting logs information into the computer. Updates concierge account, and generates any necessary invoices to either client or service vendors used.

22. White and yellow errand order sheet, driver log and other forms are all stapled together and the date and name of individual who completed the job(s) are written on the top. Forms are then filed under the client's name.

As a final note, remember that there are many concierge companies out there, and each one is unique. This is only one of the ways to set up your business. If you wish to see how the others are set up, just log onto the Internet and do a search on the word "concierge" and "errand". Read every single website, every page, and click on everything that you can possibly click on. You'll get the gist of how others are set up in no time.

Remember <u>not to sell yourself short</u>, you are a valuable person who is offering some new cutting edge services that will become invaluable to your community! If you undervalue your business, you are in effect undervaluing your services. Have faith in yourself and in the new services you are providing and you will do well. Your are offering your clients one of the most valuable things in the world - **TIME**. More time to do the things that they want to. More time to spend with their family. More time to work at their desk. More time to actually eat lunch and not run errands. More time...the ultimate commodity.

Your concierge service is the wave of the future and its cutting edge services will alleviate a lot of stress, thereby creating a more healthful environment for your client's families.

Finally, let me give you a little marketing tip. Whatever number you come up with for your yearly membership fee ... divide that number by 52. For example, $250 divided by 52 would equal $4.80 (these numbers are an example only). Your new sales pitch can now be:

"Where else can you get a personal assistant for only $4.80 per week?"

Many have have found this a great way to sell their business!

Chapter 9
Service Vendors and Commissions

Service Vendors are an important part of your business because the commissions generated build an excellent revenue source without large expenditures. Therefore, profits grow! You want to pick the cream of the crop because, to be perfectly blunt, if your service vendors do a bad job you will be the one who will ultimately take the blame for it and you might lose the client because of it. There are several steps; however, that you can follow which should allow you to avoid this pitfall.

Commissions

There are two ways to set this up. You can charge the vendor a yearly fee or you can obtain a commission. Some companies are set up to obtain commissions of 10% from each vendor, other companies in larger cities obtain commissions of 15%.

Not everyone will actually give you a commission. Legally, realtors, lawyers and financial advisors are not allowed to, and travel agents only earn about 6% per ticket they book! (You can get a commission from large groups). As a service to your clients, I think that you should still refer people to service vendors who cannot give you a commission because you will receive generous referrals from them whenever you do. The reason is that they will be grateful and will tell others about your company and the wonderful service you provide. By the way, you can also barter with them by trading your referrals for various services they can provide. However, always try to get the commission first. You can tell them that they are gaining access to your numerous and valuable clients with no advertising costs. A huge savings for them! They are gaining access to clients that they might not otherwise have!

Interviews and Contracts

It is important to not only interview service vendors that you sign on, but you should also have them sign a contract and fill out an application. Have them send you their business card and brochure for your files.

Some companies run their service vendors like a "leads group". In other words, they only put in <u>one</u> company per category (although a very complete and updated list of vendors is kept for all services). That way the service vendor is absolutely guaranteed the lead for their particular category. Interview each vendor and explain your business. Tell him/her and tell them what you expect from them ... You expect first class service from each one of them and expect them to give you 100% each time you call. In exchange for this, they receive some fantastic leads and can often double their client base within months.

There are other companies who have several vendors per

category. In this case, the interview process is the same because you still should receive first class service from each and every vendor you have sign onto your service.

All of your service vendors should completely understand that if they do not give you quality service, do not return your calls in a timely manner, or if they do not treat your clients with the respect they deserve then you will replace them with their competitor in an instant. Customer service means everything in business today, and you should give 200% to every client and service vendor that you have.

Obtaining good service vendors, however, is a full time job in itself. Ultimately, you might want to consider hiring a service vendor representative in the future, full or part time. This employee would find the service vendors, interview them and follow up with each one to obtain the commissions earned. It would be wise to have most of your service vendors on board before you open your new service up to your clients because once they start coming in your time will become even more valuable than it is now.

Where do I find the service vendors?

Ask all of your friends, family, acquaintances, and neighbors who they have used personally. Personal referrals are always the best. If you have not already done so, you can also join your local Chamber of Commerce and send out letters to service vendors explaining what you are providing, and asking them to sign on with you. I actually did a mailing like this and followed up with a telephone call and signed on some really great vendors. Once the nature of your service gets out vendors will be calling you asking to be a part of your service. You can even ask vendors who you sign on for referrals to other vendors.

Now... logistics. The vendor fills out the contract and application form and sends you a brochure and business card. You can then put their business card into a Rolodex file (or a computer database) so you can give their name to a client at a moment's notice. For this you can use two rolodex files — one round for vendors and one square for personal/general office use so that you can distinguish between the two quickly. You can also create a database in your computer for your vendors so you can find them quickly and efficiently.

List of Service Vendors

The following is a list of service vendors. I listed as many as I could think of just to get you started. This is by no means a complete list since every "service" business is a possible service vendor. The list is in alphabetical order.

- Accountant
- Air Conditioning/Heat
- Air Plane Charter

- Blinds and Curtains, window treatments
- Builder
- Carpet Cleaner
- Caterer
- Cleaning Professional
- Courier
- Decorator
- Dry Cleaner
- Electrician
- Errand Company
- Event Planner
- Financial Advisor
- "Fix-it" guy
- Florist
- Incentive Company (which sell promotional items like pens, mugs, shirts and the like)
- Insurance
- Landscaper
- Lawyer
- Maid service
- Meeting Planner
- Painter, Wallpaper Hanger
- Personal Chef
- Personnel Company
- Pet-Related Companies like veterinarians, pet-sitters and hidden fence companies
- Photographer
- Plumber
- Printer
- Realtor

- Sign maker
- Special Event Company
- Transportation Company (limousine, bus, town car, taxi service and the like)
- Trophy/Award/Plaque maker

How do I get the Commissions from the Vendors?

Logistically, there are thousands of ways to set this up. Most likely, you will have to negotiate with each vendor that you sign up to find out the method that works best for you. Here are some ways that others have set it up. Personally, I prefer the first but I have seen companies have success with all three methods.

1. You can take all the orders yourself. For example, you would advertise the same price that your vendor charges, arrange for the job, the client would pay you and you would pay the vendor. Then, when you actually do pay the vendor you would deduct the 10-15% commission from the total.

2. You can charge your clients 10-15% more than the vendor's advertised prices.

3. You can outsource it completely to the vendor and let him and your client make the arrangements. Then, a few days after the job is supposed to be completed you call the client and find out how it went. At the end of the month you send the vendor an invoice for the appropriate commissions.

Whichever one you use, please <u>make sure</u> that you get everything in writing detailing the fee structure as completely as possible.

On the next page, you will find a sample vendor proposal for your convenience when creating your own letter. Further, a sample vendor application can be found at the end of the book.

Sample Vendor Proposal

Date

Mr. Stan Vendor
7027 ABC Road
Charlotte, NC 22222

Dear Stan:

As per our recent telephone conversation, Sample Concierge would like to add your business services to our member Business Referral List.

In short, we are Sample City's new personal assistant and meeting/event/travel planner. We are dedicated to giving our clients back one of their most valuable possessions...time. Rather than spend part of their busy workday ordering flowers, planning vacations, checking airfares, ordering transportation (train, plane, bus, limousine), ordering tickets or leaving early to pick up dry cleaning and groceries you can now call us to do these tiresome tasks for you. Sample Concierge is a one-stop shop where you can send us your "to do" list and then consider it done!

Our **Business Referral Service** works like this... Clients are more than welcome to access our business referral service and obtain a referral for virtually anything. Business such as childcare, Maids and and Cleaning Professionals, Mechanics, Plumbers, Electricians, Realtors, Builders, Architects, Petcare, Landscapers, Wallpaper Hangers, Painters, Carpet Cleaners, Locksmiths, Health and Fitness Clubs, Moving Companies and more.

If you would like to join our service vendor list, then please fill out the attached forms and send them to us. We do ask for a reasonable 10% commission for every referral we send you, but don't worry if your business is not set up for this. As part of our services to our clients we always follow up with them to find out if they were completely satisfied with the vendors that we referred them to. This helps us to provide the very best to our clients plus it keeps our best vendors at the top of our referral list.

If you wish to check us out then please visit our website at www.sampleconcierge.com. You can also call us at 555-555-5555. Thank you and I look forward to hearing from you soon.

Sincerely,

Joseph Van Pelt
President

"Nothing great was ever achieved without enthusiasm."

Ralph Waldo Emerson

Chapter 10
Errand Service

There are two ways to set this up. First you could outsource it to a local errand service company and obtain a commission on each run they make, or, you could do it yourself. If there is no errand company to outsource it to in your area, or you just want to do it yourself because of the additional revenue that you can make, here's how to set it up.

Finding the Drivers/Personal Shoppers

Placing an ad in your local paper's classified section will work. Another source for reliable staff can be found at local senior centers. Visit in person and ask if any seniors might want to run some errands to earn a little extra cash. They are reliable, honest and very hard workers! You can also use stay-at-home mothers who want to work part time.

The drivers must be neat, presentable, and clean. You can require them to wear Kacki pants or shorts and a collared shirt. Each car can receive two magnetic signs for their car doors as well as business cards and brochures to hand out along the way. They are generally paid by the hour and full time drivers are eligible for benefits. Many companies provide their drivers with a company car to drive, which is a great idea once you have the financial base to pay for it. Drivers should

also have a company ID clearly showing the client that they
are your representative or employee.

Should I hire them as Independent contractors or employees?

A very good question! Here is a brief answer ...

Independent contractors are not employees so you will not have
to pay them the worker's compensation or benefits that you are
required to pay an employee. You are also not liable for any
negligent acts that they commit. If you hire a courier to take a
box across town, for example, you are not liable for any damage
or injuries that might happen during the course of the delivery
of the box. If, on the other hand, the courier is an employee
driving a company car, then you are responsible for anything
that might happen. At the end of the year, you will be
responsible for giving them the appropriate 1099 for their taxes
(you should contact your accountant for the details on 1099's).
The downside here is that you don't have any real control over
"when" and "how" they are going to work.

Employees, on the other hand, can be required to wear certain
clothes, have set work hours and a specific number of sick and
vacation days. You can train them how to treat your clients
and teach them the skills they need to perform their duties in
order to maintain consistency within your company. You can
teach and hire loyal, honest and reliable employees. With

independent contractors you might not be able to establish any
of these as they are not your employee. I am not saying that
contractors won't be honest and reliable, I am merely pointing
out that they won't be as loyal to you as an employee will.

If you need more information on this topic, then I suggest that
you contact your lawyer or your certified public accountant.

Setting it up

In the beginning you will find yourself doing most of the
errands. Hire people one at a time increasing your staff as you
increase your sales and revenue. Give each driver either a cell
phone or a beeper so that you can contact them with changes or
additions to their schedule.

Ideally, there should be one person in the office "dispatching"
all the drivers, not to mention to get more business and make
"sales" calls. In addition, try to coordinate drivers so that they
may be able to run errands or shop for more than one customer
at a time. For example, perhaps you have three clients and you
have told the first client that her errands will take about 2
hours. The other two clients have been told that their errands
will take one hour each. 4 Hours on errands total. By
combining the errands for these three people, the driver could
potentially complete the errands in 3 hours thereby saving
time and increasing revenue.

Have the drivers keep ALL receipts and record EVERY errand they go on. Each driver should record exactly where they go and how much they spend on the daily trip sheet form (sample enclosed). They can either carry cash to pay for the errands or a company credit/debt card. If possible, set up credit with the businesses that your company uses most often.

It is probably easiest in the long run to set up your business so that you can accept credit cards. Then your customer can give you their credit card to keep on file and you can charge whatever errands you run for them to the card. If, however, you are not set up for credit cards you can create a concierge account for them before you run the errand. For example, Mrs. Smith wants you to pick up some groceries, go to the drug store and post office, buy some special food for the dog at the vet's and then run to the frame store to buy a few frames for some pictures she has. You should ask her to deposit $100 into her concierge account. Then, you use this money to run the errand and you can either bill her for the balance (if there is any), or she can pay you on the spot with a check when you deliver her supplies. You can also ask each client to keep a minimum balance in their account (like $200 for example) to use to pay for the errands.

If you plan on actually going into people's homes, then it will be helpful for you to keep a key-rack of some sort in your office since many clients prefer you to keep a copy of their key so they don't have to be bothered.

A very nice touch is to send each client a personal thank you note after they use your service. We have a carpet cleaner who sends us a handwritten thank you note after he cleans our carpets! This personalized touch keeps me from using anyone else and I have referred him to more people than I can count.

I also suggest that you have each employee sign a non-competition clause. The last thing you want to do is to train your competitors!

Accepting Credit Cards — E-commerce

We have done a great deal of research on this topic and have looked into a bunch of companies that will set you up to accept credit cards. It is an ideal way to do business because clients find it easier to just give you their credit card number to pay for services as opposed to giving you a check.

There are many different credit card services and banks who will help you set up your merchant account so that you can begin to accept credit cards. You can accept Visa, Mastercard, American Express, Discover Card and you can buy, lease equipment or do it via the web. We suggest that you do yourself a favor and do some research and comparison-shopping. Look around and see what the best deal is! Look up the word "merchant account" in the yellow pages, on the internet or ask someone you know for a referral. Ask your bank as they might have a great program available.

128

Do the research to find the best rates and fees, but please do not forget about service! The lowest fees for a service might not be the best one for your service as they might not be able to meet your specific needs.

A good place to start your research is the company that we use, AIS Media (www.aismedia.com). Please check them out and the many others that are available to you. Then you can make an informed decision on what will be right for you and your clients.

Chapter 11
Staff

In the beginning, you are the staff. Once you get your business up and running, however, you will have to hire people to help you. I suggest that you hire one person at a time according to your budget. As your gross sales increase, your staff can increase.

In a perfect world you might have the following (just to name a few):

1. Errand Drivers/Personal Shoppers
2. Bookkeeper and/or accountant (which can be done yourself with software)
3. A person to work with the service vendors. He/she would find the vendor, interview them, and get them to sign the contract and follow-up with them to obtain the commissions.
4. In-house concierges answering and filling all the requests that come in via e-mail, phone and fax.
5. Sales/Marketing person
6. Lobby concierges as necessary
7. Operations Manager
8. Office Manager
9. Secretary and/or Administrative Assistant

Remember that a happy employee will work harder and stay longer so I suggest you try and be as "family friendly" as possible. Work out a flexible schedule whether it is for a sick child or to attend a school performance. As long as they get their work done it should be no problem to accommodate your staff. If you need them to work with you until 9 pm at night why not buy them a little dinner or order in a pizza? Treat your employees as you would treat your own family. Treat them like you would like to be treated if you were in their shoes. In fact, put yourself in their shoes and ask yourself "what would I want and how would I want to be treated?"

Putting honesty, integrity, and love first will only help increase your business. Nice guys DO finish first. If you are honest, ethical and trustworthy about everything that you do, not only will you receive repeat business from your clients, but you will also get 110% from your staff.

Of course I would not shoot myself in the foot either. Run both a state and federal background check on each of your employees. Go down to your local police department and ask them to run it for you. It is very inexpensive and well worth it. I would also run a credit check on each employee. Your employees need to be as honest as you are. If they see a $1000 bill on a client's kitchen table when they come in, it should be there when they leave.

The Hiring Process

Here are a few tips to help you minimize hiring mistakes.

First you need to complete a profile of the perfect employee. Determine what skills and personal characteristics you wish them to have. Do NOT become desperate (even if you feel like you are) because it will only cause you to lower your standards and will lead you to believe that someone is qualified when they are not. Hiring incompetent people will just make everyone unhappy and will ultimately lead to problems.

Make up a list of "must have" and "would like to have". List those qualities that are related to skills, educational and work experience, behavior, and personality that you would like your idea candidate to have. Use this list to ask open-ended questions in the interview. For example, "Can you describe to me the last time you handled an angry customer?"

Pay attention to the way they dress. Are they neat and clean? Were they on-time for the interview? Are they sitting in the chair leaning forward or are they slumped back? When they talk about their past job which word do they use more frequently "I" or "we"? Using "we" indicates someone is a team player.

After the interview, if possible, have a co-worker or your business partner take the candidate to lunch. Their guard will be down and they will be more apt to behave naturally.

Once you hire the employee make sure they get off to a great start and be prepared for them. If they get off to a good start they will be motivated contributors from day one. Have their business cards ready and desk all set up. Everything they need should be ready by the time they arrive for their first day at work. Assign them a "buddy" to help them their first week. Ideally, this person would introduce them to your staff, give them a tour of the office, take them to lunch, fill them in on the company culture, and answer all their questions. Of course, if they are your first or second employee then you will be the buddy!

Finally, as boss you should meet with your new employee at the end of each day for the first week to make sure they are settling in ok and address any questions they might have. Letting a newly hired employee know how valuable they are from the beginning will only help you and is a really great company policy to have.

Chapter 12
Meeting and Event Planning

There is so much involved in meeting and event planning that the topic could take its own book to fully describe. However, in the interests of time and space this chapter will only briefly discuss the major details. If you wish to learn more about this topic check the resource library on the Meeting Professionals International's webpage at www.mpiweb.org. There are some really excellent guides available to help you prepare for meeting planning.

Potential scenario: A client calls your office requesting help planning their daughter's wedding. A few minutes later a second client calls asking for help planning their annual Holiday party and a third client wants to have a meeting for some out-of-town clients.

In this industry, you have three very distinct choices here:

1. You call an independent meeting/event planner and farm the events out to them. Meeting planners generally charge anywhere from $50 -$250 per hour for their services, and you should receive a 10% commission on the total price charged to the client.
2. You farm out one or two of the events to the independent meeting planner and you do the third one yourself.

3. You do all of the events yourself and keep the fee.

The most lucrative choice, of course, would be to do everything yourself. However, if you have never planned a meeting in your life the task can be daunting. Here are a few simple tips that will make your life easier. For further information, check out the library at Meeting Professionals International www.mpiweb.org. Each of the following topics is discussed in detail with a complete list of resources. This list is intended to only help you get started.

Budgets and Clients - getting started

The first thing you need to do is to obtain some basic information from the client.

1. What kind of function is it? Birthday, wedding, anniversary, company picnic, office party, seminar, meeting, networking reception, or exhibit?
2. How much do they want to spend? Obtain a budget for the event
3. How many people will be there?
4. When do they want to have it - date and time of the event?
5. Where do they want to have it? Hotel, restaurant, convention center?
6. Do they want it centered around a theme of some kind, a company logo, a specific season or perhaps even a specific color?
7. Do they need entertainment? If yes, what kind?

8. Is it a food function? If yes, sit-down or buffet? Full meal or Hors d'oeuvres?

9. Will invitations need to be sent out? If yes, do they want help?

10. Will they need flowers, decorations or a photographer?

Once the client furnishes you with this information, you can begin to find a location for the event.

Site Selection — How to find the site

Once I have obtained the preliminary information from my client I gather together a list of properties that I think would work for them. Then I call each property to check for availability. If the site is available I make an appointment with the sales manager tour the property and discuss the perspective event.

I have a rule that has served me well during the 15 years I have been a meeting planner.

Never book a property without seeing it first!

Always do a site inspection of the property before you suggest it or sign any contracts because you need to know if the location will work for your client. Taking a few of your own photographs can also be helpful if clients are unable to visit to location for themselves.

How do I find the properties? Both your local Chamber of
Commerce and your Convention and Visitors Bureau (CV&B)
will be able to help you. If you give your local CV&B the
details of the event they will find some properties for you —
FREE! This is a truly valuable resource and one I use
frequently.   The yellow pages can also be useful by looking
under topics such as hotels, motels, conventions and
restaurants. Valuable listings can also be found on the
Internet. By conducting a search through your local city

Once at the site, there are several key things that I look for.

1. Is it clean, neat and orderly? Nicely decorated? Did
   someone greet you when you arrived?
2. Is the meeting room or event space large enough for your
   group? Is it nicely furnished?
3. Where is the kitchen? If it's on another floor the food might
   be cold by the time it arrives. Also if the kitchen is directly
   on the other side of the room you're meeting in, be careful. I
   once booked a meeting in NYC in a really nice hotel only to
   find the kitchen was just on the other side of the wall. All
   during the meeting you could hear dishes rattling, carts
   rolling around, people talking – it was very disruptive.
4.   Do they have an in-house audio-visual department or will
   you have to hire one outside.
5.   Where are the bathrooms and how many are there? I'm not

kidding about this one. I know someone who once booked a meeting for 1,000 people and forgot to check this. Once there, she found out that there was one ladies room with only three stalls! You can only imagine what happened!

6. Are there telephones nearby? How many? Where are they?

7. If a hotel, what about the sleeping rooms? Are they nicely furnished? How large are they? Are they clean? Is the rug clean? Bathroom? What kinds of amenities come with it - hairdryers, irons and ironing boards? Can a person hook up their laptop?

8. If some of your client's guests will be coming from out-of-town, you need to find out how far the property is from the airport and public transportation. Do they have a shuttle?

9. Ask the salesperson when they plan on updating, redecorating the property. The last thing you want is your people to be greeted by a construction site!

10. What type of deposit do they require? What is their cancellation policy?

11. Are there going to be any other major groups or conventions in town that week?

12. Sit in the lobby for a while and just observe. Are the guests greeted and taken care of as quickly as possible? Is the luggage taken care of quickly? Is there a line for the elevator or are there plenty of elevator banks to handle all the guests? This is another one of those "it happened to me" kind of stories. I booked a conference in Seattle WA for 1100 people and there was always a long wait for the elevators! We got complaints left and right from everyone

so I always make a point of seeing how many elevators the property has.

13. Is there plenty of parking for guests?
14. Is the property accessible for the handicapped?

I generally will present my client with a choice of 3 properties, with my first choice listed at the top. I will include all the brochures and prices from each property and present it to the client in proposal form. Now it is up to the client to choose. Once they do, you can begin negotiating the contract with the facility. Once negotiated, the client should sign the contract, not you. This way if the meeting is canceled or something goes wrong, the hotel will hold your client responsible and not you.

Contracts

Hotel contracts may look simple on the outside, but many have some clauses on the inside that could give you a major headache. If you cancel the event, find out from the salesperson exactly what you will be charged for. Some hotels will charge you for all the "lost revenue" that your group **might have** provided had the meeting not been cancelled, and the wording is so vague in the contract that you might never find it. This means that the hotel can charge you for things like food, room service, room nights, and telephone calls. So, make sure the contract CLEARLY states what you will be charged for in case of cancellation. If a detailed description is not there, make them add it in before your client signs.

The contract should also clearly define the scope of the meeting, location of where the function is to be, date of the function and the function requirements. If there is only one room in the whole place that will suit your needs, MAKE SURE THEY WRITE IT IN! Otherwise, the facility has the right to put you wherever they deem appropriate. Of course, this is easier said than done, since many facilities will flat out refuse to do this. In this case, find out where they would move you and then decide if you can live with it. If not, go somewhere else.

Also, try and get them to guarantee their food and beverage prices. If your event is months away, the chance that their food and beverage prices will go up is pretty high. So choose the menu BEFORE you sign the contract and get them to lock in their current prices.

Find out what group, if any, is going to be in there at the same time. What if you are having a wedding and the Oklahoma State Marching Band is having band practice right next door? Or, what if you are having a business meeting and there is a huge church revival with lots of singing taking place in the next room? These examples are obviously not likely to occur, but I am sure you get the point.

You can purchase our meeting/event planning contract that we use with our clients by simply going to our website. Again, be sure to have your own lawyer look it over before you use it.

To recap what we've done so far: we've discussed with our client what kind of party they want; established how much they wish to pay; and determined the date and general location for the event. Using these criteria we put together a list of possible sites for the function. We visited each site and presented our client with a list of the top three sites to choose from. The contract was negotiated and signed by the client. Now we are ready to move onto the next step.... logistics.

Logistics - Creating the Event

What exactly is logistics? Logistics are the nitty gritty details that go into planning an event. They include things like choosing the menu, typing up the name-tags, addressing the invitations, setting up the function room, calling the speakers to find out what their special needs are, and arranging for the audio visual equipment.

Let's take this one topic at a time.

Food and Beverage

The first thing you should do is find out if your client has a preference as to what to serve. If they do not, then offer suggestions based on their budget, guests and what the location has to offer. Put yourself in their shoes, if you were one of the attendees what would you want to eat?

As mentioned earlier, you also need to consider their budget. For example, if you are planning a wedding, then it might not be cost effective to hire the best caterer in town because of all the other costs involved. Remember the most expensive is not necessarily the best. If you are hiring a caterer then shop around. Ask your friends and neighbors who they have used in the past. Ask the caterer if you can sample their food. Ask for references and call them.

If you are working with a hotel, then the catering manager will be able to find you something suitable that is well within your budget. Remember that you don't necessarily have to stick to what they have on their menu. You can usually substitute things and work with the hotel's Chef to design a meal that meets all your requirements and fits within your budget.

Here are some tricks of the trade that will keep your costs down:

1. For a breakfast, cut your breakfast pastries in half.
2. For a lunch, serve the dessert at your afternoon break. This is a great way to keep people awake during the afternoon because it gives them a little sugar boost and prevents you from having to buy something to go with the coffee and soda in the afternoon.
3. At a buffet, make sure the plates are small so the guests don't load up. Some people will make the reception their dinner and will eat as much as possible so they can save

money by not going to a restaurant.

4. Serve "dead stock wine" with the meal. Many hotels will routinely change their house wines from time to time and they might still have a few bottles of the "old" house wine left in their basement. So ask them about it! If they have some they will generally offer it to you at a discounted price.

5. If you must have a full bar at a reception then have a waiter standing at the entrance offering glasses of wine and silver platters of food to the guests as they walk in. Most people will not drink hard liquor once they have started with wine. The beauty of this is that it will create a very elegant atmosphere at your function. Waiters decked out in tuxedos and white gloves are a nice addition to any event.

6. Only pay for the bottles that have been opened. If you have a lot of half-full bottles left over at the end of the reception don't forget to take them home with you! You paid for them!

7. Have the bartenders measure each drink as opposed to free pouring.

8. Don't put the food on tables near the entrance. Instead put them at the back of the room so people have to search for them.

9. Have each food station manned by a waiter. Most people will not pile their plates high with food if someone is watching them.

10. If you are in a hotel, find out what other groups are serving and offer the same thing. The hotel will give you a discount

because they will be able to buy in bulk.

11. Try to make sure that the coffee break gets put outside of the room in the hall and not inside the room. The rattling of dishes and coffee cups can be very distracting.

12. Serve finger food at coffee breaks. There is nothing worse than trying to do a balancing act with your coffee cup and plate while trying to hold a conversation with someone. Keep it simple and elegant.

13. Don't forget about serving pasta and salad for lunch instead of the proverbial "rubber chicken". It is generally less expensive than other food items and people love it.

14. If your client wishes the function to have a theme of some kind, ask the hotel if they have any decorations in their basement that is leftover from previous groups.

15. Ask the hotel if you can "borrow" some of the plants from their lobby to use at your reception.

A really nice touch for out-of-town attendees at a meeting is to organize a dinner for them. Collect the menus from one or two local restaurants and mention to your clients that you will be calling them later in the day to make a group reservation. Then, place a sign up sheet near the registration area so that people can sign up to go to one of the restaurants for a "Dutch treat" dinner of networking and fun. Also, make sure the group's leader informs the group about the sign up sheet during the morning announcements. At about 3:00 pm close the sign-up sheets and call in the reservation. Everyone has a great time at these things. When traveling, I generally will not go out to a restaurant because I really hate to eat alone. I prefer to eat in my room if I have no one to go with. This solves this same problem for everyone. You can go out to a great restaurant and network with the other attendees while having a great time. Try it!

Registration - Nametags

If you are planning a meeting of some kind, then chances are pretty good you will want each attendee to wear a nametag. You have two choices here:

1. You can have some blank "sticky" badges at a table by the entrance and the attendee can write their own badge.
2. You can offer each attendee a pre-printed computerized badge.

If you choose the latter, the company that we use is **pc/ nametag**. To get a copy of their catalogue you can call them at 1-800-233-9767. They have some really excellent computer software systems for badges that are both versatile and reasonable. You can also find badge stock, plastic pin cases, ribbons and other items that will help make your meetings look professional.

Registration - Location and Staff

If you have to register people and hand out badges, then make sure that the registration table is easy to find. Don't put it in an out-of-the way coatroom. Place it directly outside your main meeting room so that attendees can find it quickly and easily. Directional signs placed in the lobby are also helpful.

For a small group (up to 50) you will need at least one 8-ft. table and a few chairs for the staff to sit on. However, if your client is handing out some material you will need at least one additional table to place it on.

Expect to use an additional table for every 50 people. Larger groups should be divided alphabetically. If money is to be taken at the door, keep paid registration separate from the unpaid. It helps to make the lines go quicker. It is also a good idea to have a separate "information" table so that people can ask questions without slowing down the line.

Also make sure that there are some comfortable seats for the attendees to sit on. Many like to get their registration materials and then go sit down and look at it. Complimentary beverages are also a nice touch if it is within the budget.

The local Convention and Visitors Bureau can also set up a table where people can get information on restaurants, tours, general information and maps of the area. This also adds a nice touch.

Your staff should be dressed in business attire and should be friendly and smiling. Remember that they will be representing your company and will be the first people that attendees see, so they must appear professional at all times. In fact, your local Convention and Visitors Bureau will be able to find you some registration personnel if you don't wish to tie up your own staff. These people are always well-trained and wonderful to work with!

Photographers, Florists, Decorations

Ask the client if they will be needing any photographers, videographers, press coverage, flower arrangements, speaker tables and/or registration tables. A very nice thing to do is to place a sticker under ONE coffee cup at each table. The person who gets the sticker gets to take home the flower arrangement at their table. Another great thing to do at banquets and/or weddings is to place a disposable camera at each table. You can get some really wonderful candid pictures that the event's official photographer can't.

If your client has a theme or any special colors, ask the catering manager for your event if you have any choices for tablecloth color and decorations. You can also ask the catering manager what themes they have done in the past for other clients to get an idea of what might work for your group.

Don't forget about the invitations to the event! You can design a nice brochure or flyer that outlines the details of the function and gives information about where to send registration money, or, you can send out hand-written invitations. It really all depends on the type of function you are having.

Entertainment

Is there a special theme for the event? Perhaps a local trio of wandering musicians to greet the guests would be fun, or a magician wandering around doing tricks? Call your local CV&B for entertainment suggestions since they always have the inside track! (yes, I use them a lot can you tell?) Local speaker bureaus can also give you some wonderful leads for entertainment. The catering manager for your event will also be a valuable resource for you because, remember, they've done this before hundreds of times! So don't be afraid to ask questions because that is what they're there for.

Before you finish making your plans, don't forget about security! If you have to store things overnight make sure the facility has a safe place for you to keep them. Are there going to be any VIP's that require additional security attending the meeting? Don't forget to ask your client! How about press coverage?

Planning a meeting or event doesn't have to be hard; it is just time consuming. When you think of something, write it down on a pad on your desk. Meeting planning is simply organizing the details for other people. Take things one at a time and keep yourself organized and you will do just fine. Write down exactly what you have to do and check off the items as you go because you will be less likely to forget something along the way.

Chapter 13
Sales and Marketing

Now that you've set your business up you are ready to start
work. Let the phone begin to ring! The following chapter is
filled with some useful tips to help you get started with the
sales and marketing.

Know your Business

This may sound redundant but it is also true. Know your
business. Be able to "talk the talk". Know it inside, outside,
backwards and upside down. You should, by now, be able to
talk about every aspect of your business to anyone who asks.
Energy and excitement should creep into your voice as you
explain it to people. They should both feel and see your energy
as you talk and "sell" to them. Show your excitement!

Now don't get me wrong, I am not suggesting that you leap
around the room doing back flips, I am merely suggesting that
you don't hold back your excitement. Your excitement will
infuse their excitement. Your positive energy will cause their
positive energy. Talk to everyone you know about it - your
neighbors, family, everyone. Network with everyone because
everyone is a possible client. Get excited!

It also helps to have some facts and figures to use in your

conversation. Feel free to use the figures I included in the introduction to this book since it will demonstrate your knowledge of your business.

Professional Image

There are three things that you need as a sales professional. The first is the proper clothing, and I can't stress this enough because you want the client to remember your service NOT what you wore. This also does not necessarily mean a business suit. You should be clean and neat. Your style of clothing depends of what service you are providing. For example, if you were pitching a corporate client or real estate management company then I would suggest suitable business attire. If, on the other hand, you are running errands on behalf of the company then I suggest pants and a collared shirt of some kind, perhaps with your company logo on it. Anything you wear should be clean, neat and wrinkle-free.

Speech

You also need to speak and write well. If you mumble, ramble on and don't have a clear command of the language then you will not be taken seriously. You will have to have both one-on-one conversations as well as group presentations. If you want corporate clients then most likely you will be asked to present your services to them at their next business meeting. Many community colleges and universities offer non-credit courses in public speaking. There are also some really wonderful books written on the subject.

The written word is also very important because it is our written word that people most often see first in brochures, sales letters, webpage and in the sales kit. There are some nice software programs out there that will help you edit your letters and text as well as some really great books. Taking the time to be a better writer is worth it.

Manners and Etiquette

There is more to this than just putting your napkin in your lap, not slurping your soup and not interrupting. You will be required to not only hold conversations with people, but will have to dine with them on occasion, meet them in their homes and make introductions. Being honest, sincere, friendly and polite is a major part of concierge work. Good manners will not help increase your clientele but it will help prevent embarrassing moments that may lose them.

Take the time to learn the customs and culture of your international clients to make them feel more comfortable and to prevent any embarrassing slip-ups. For example, when you are given a business card from a Japanese Client it is important to accept the card with both hands and bow in acceptance. Do NOT write anything on the card as they consider this extremely rude.

The Handshake

I know what you're thinking "handshake? Now she's gone too
far!" Well, hear me out first. The following article was written
for exhibitors at a trade show but actually applies to everyone
even remotely associated with sales. The data suggests that
just this small simple gesture can make a world of difference to
your results. Furthermore, make sure that you look directly
into their eyes when you shake their hand because eye contact
is just as important.

Put it There
By Dr. Allen Konopacki

In an age where the word communication conjures up images of
phone lines and video screens, a trade show seems like the one
place where meeting in person is still an important concept.
The success of the trade show industry proves that even in a
world where technology reigns supreme, nothing is as effective
as face-to-face contact.

Yet a new study suggests that exhibitors are leaving out a key
element for making in-person meetings valuable: the
handshake. The study, conducted by the Incomm Center for
Trade Show Research, found that in theory, practice and fact a
little shake of the hand goes a very long way toward giving
your booth a boost.

Theory

Why do handshakes matter? They create warmth, trust and a sense of an immediate mutual relationship. They are also a great way to make your exhibit stand out from the others. **People tend to remember a person who greets them with a handshake more than those who don't**, and they'll be more likely to return to that person's booth because they felt welcome.

The first time you greet someone is critical because a relationship is usually established in the first four seconds of contact. There's an art to working trade shows successfully, and using a handshake can create a positive impression that can eventually win you sales.

Practice

To better understand the importance of handshakes, the following experiment was conducted for the study. A group of students left a quarter in a public phone booth. After strangers used the phone and took the coin, one of the students walked up to ask if they had seen the quarter. Of the roughly 75 people who were approached, over 40 lied, saying that they had never seen the 25 cents they had pocketed.

The experiment was then tried with another group of 75 strangers, with the difference being that the student greeted the person with a quick handshake and an introduction, then asked if the quarter had been spotted. Of this group, the number of people who fibbed dropped to 18 of the 75.

The conclusion was simple: handshakes create a higher degree of intimacy and trust within a matter of seconds. In fact, the gesture carries perhaps more weight than ever because so many face-to-face encounters have been replaced by phone calls, faxes and e-mail. A handshake is perceived as being reserved for personal attention.

Fact

Examples are all fine and good, but the evidence that handshakes have an actual effect is based on hard numbers. Here are the industry facts:

Only 8 percent of exhibit sales representatives greet visitors to a trade show exhibit with a handshake. Even worse, the typical greetings used by salespeople, such as "Can I answer any questions?" or "May I help you?" are impersonal, and thus reduce comfort and trust.

When greeted with a handshake, 76 percent of individuals respond by being more open, friendly and honest. Salespeople who shake hands with a prospect or customer are twice as likely to be remembered compared to those salespeople who don't shake hands. In short, handshakes build a higher degree of interaction and memorability.

Reprinted with permission from trade show ideas, a publication of the Trade Show Exhibitors Association, 5501 Backlick Rd., Ste. 105, Springfield, VA 22151, 709-941-3725.

Sales Presentation

You might be asked to make a sales presentation to a corporate client. GREAT! Be prepared and know your client and you will do fine. Remember that you are selling an intangible service. A service that many people have never heard of or even considered. It is your job to bring this service to life through your presentation and enthusiasm. The following tips can be used for both one-on-one presentations and group.

1. Make sure each attendee at the meeting has something to hold in their hands like a sales kit or your brochure.
2. Customize the materials inside of the kit as much as possible by putting the client's name on it as much as possible. Make sure the information is updated and fresh.
3. Directly relate your service to the client's business. How your service will directly affect their employees. What your service will do to make their job easier. Also explain how your service works.
4. Research the company for facts and figures to add to your presentation. It always pays to do your homework. If you are pitching a real estate management company, visit their properties and see which ones can have a lobby concierge.
5. Get the client involved. Ask them to turn to another page. Get them to ask questions.
6. Know the result you want...plan for the outcome. What do you want the presentation to accomplish? Do you want to just introduce your service or do you want them to actually

sign a contract with you?

7. If applicable, create a short slide show so they have something to look at while you speak.

8. Create a list of possible objections the client might have and prepare an answer for each one.

9. Ask the client if there is any reason this service might not work for them. It is better to get everything onto the table all at once so you can address each issue rather than leave with them hanging in the air. Try the "feel, felt, found" method — I know how you feel, I felt the same way, but what I have found is this... This method allows them to not feel bullied into accepting something they're not sure they want

10. Be friendly. Smile. Maintain eye contact and listen to their replies. Lean forward instead of leaning back and relaxing. Look excited! Take notes. Think before you speak!

11. When closing you can either give them a few alternatives or be completely honest and direct and ask for the business outright. **Ask for the business**, the worst thing that they can say to you is no.

12. Follow up with the client and be reachable through e-mail, fax and cell-phone. Make sure to thank them for their time!!

13. Make sure that your return <u>ALL</u> telephone calls and e-mails within 24 hours. Don't burn your bridges with this one. If it's a sales call that you really don't want to return just remember that you never know who they might know and can refer your company to. What if they happen to be

the daughter of IBM's president? You just never know. So do what I do, return everyone's call within 24 hours no matter who they are.

14. Finally, show them your dependability by following through with any request that they might make.

Chapter 14

30 Ways to Grow Your Concierge Business without spending a fortune!

The first step in growing your new business is to find the customers. Pretty basic right? You must continue to generate new business or your business will fail. Here are some tips on where to find them. Please note that not every tip will work for everyone. It really depends on both the type of service you have and who you are marketing to. Persistence is the key here! Don't give up after only one or two tries because it might take more. Remember that you are selling an intangible service that everyone needs, but none of them think that they need it, so it is up to you to convince them of its value — and this takes time.

1. **Join your local Chamber of Commerce and go to all their networking functions.**

   The key here is to network, network, network! Talk to everyone that you can about your new business. Hand out your business cards to everyone you meet! I like the cards that are folded where your information appears on the top and a quick list of your services is inside - a sort of mini-brochure.

2. **Purchase the Chamber's mailing list and send out your brochure, business card and a short letter to each member.**

    The cost will range in price from $20 to $200 depending upon where you live. Follow each letter up with a telephone call. You can also use your local yellow pages or any mailing list from your marketing area.

3. **Develop a mailing list and send them a mailing every month.**

    Develop a newsletter and send it out every other month. Send out special gift certificates or two-for-one dinner special coupons from a local restaurant. You need to stay in front of someone at least 10 times before they will respond to you so persistence is the key with marketing.

4. **Create a webpage**

    Triangle Concierge gets 99% of its clients from our website and from referrals. Your website will enable thousands of people to find about you and your new service quickly and easily. Remember, however, that once created you MUST submit your site to search engines at least once a month. If they cannot find you when doing a search then your website is not working for you.

5. Call local corporations in your area about your new service.

When calling a corporation do <u>NOT</u> call the human resource department...more often than not they will not return your call and you will only get more and more frustrated. Instead call the gatekeeper. The gatekeeper holds the key to the company. Who is this marvelous person you ask? The President or CEO's secretary. Let's call her Betty. Once Betty is on the line ask her if she could do you a favor. Now most people experience a knee jerk reaction to this question and will say, "yes of course, what can I do for you?"

You then <u>briefly</u> tell Betty what service you are providing and ask her if she could tell you whom you could talk to within the company. Remember to keep it brief, she is NOT who you are selling the service to. She will most likely then give you a name (John Smith, for example). You thank her profusely and then end the call. You then call John Smith. When he answers you simply tell him that Betty Jones gave you his name and go into your 30 second presentation.

After this call, please don't forget to write Betty a handwritten thank you note, or send her a gift certificate for errand hours because it *was* thoughtful of her to give you the name, and it will keep your company name inside of her head so that when she sees it again she will remember you.

6. **Cold call local real estate management companies to offer lobby concierge services.**

7. **Send out a press release to all the newspapers, television and radio stations in your area announcing your new business.**

   This is one of the best ways to grow your business — and it doesn't cost you a cent to do!

8. **Place an ad in your local yellow pages.**

9. **Stuff resident mailboxes with a flyer.**

10. **Place an ad in your local papers and magazines**

11. **Go to every networking function you can find. Attend all the local expositions and hand your business card out to everyone you can. Network, network, and network!**

12. **Trade Shows**

   You can either be one of the exhibitors at a local exposition, or you may simply attend one and hand out business cards to everyone you meet. Both are valuable. It is also a nice way to obtain service vendors for a business referral service.

13. Ask the owner of a local coffee shop if you can put some brochures on his counter.

I have many clients who have told me that this is one of the best ways they have found to grow their business.

14. Collect business cards. Make contact with anyone in the corporate environment.

15. Place flyers in business journals or newspapers.

16. Seminars: Either taking them or giving them.
Enrolling in some business, sales or marketing courses can lead to some very effective networking as well as teach you a new thing or two. Also, making a presentation at a seminar can make you an "expert" in your field.

17. Place signs on every errand running vehicle.

18. Read the business section of your local newspaper and look for company and personal leads

19. Ask people for leads and contacts.

20. Visit your local spas

Propose that they include errand running with their all-day packages. As the clients get pampered, you run their errands for them! By the end of the day not only do they feel great, but their errands are all done. This idea would also work for hair and nail salons.

21. Contact local surgeons.

Often they will send home a patient with orders for com-plete and total bed rest. And, if that patients spouse cannot boil water then its trouble! Offer 1 or 2 hour errand gift certificates that the surgeon can give to his/her patients who are recovering from surgery. Also, the surgeons them-selves (as well as the nurses) are notoriously busy people and might benefit from your new service.

22. Go to your local country club or golf course

Offer to make your services a part of one of their member-ship packages. Logistics are great because 9 times out of 10 the member lives within a 5-mile radius of the club. An-other good idea is to offer a golf package - tee off and gives us your "to do" list. When you reach the 18th hole your errands are done and in the trunk of your car ready to go!

23. Affiliate with a local professional organizer com-pany.

Many professional organizers will have a client that not only needs help with organizing their lives, but with their daily tasks as well.

24. Get to know some local realtors ... notoriously busy people!

25. How about the airport?

Pilots and airline attendants are away for days at a time and might need a little helping hand once in a while.

26. Contact travel agencies
Ask them about offering pet-sitting or house-sitting services to their out-of-town clients.

27. Previous colleagues and associates.

Remember the people you used to work with in your last job? Remember how you liked each other? Well somehow over the years you have lost track of them. Now is the time to re-kindle those lost friendships. Watch where they lead ... you might be surprised! Add them to your mailing list to keep in touch with them. Your new newsletter is a great way to keep in touch with them.

28. Build your own in-house mailing list

An in-house mailing list will produce, on average, 5 to 10 times the response of any outside mailing lists that you use.

Get the names from business cards you have obtained,
membership lists from organizations that you belong to,
your Rolodex file, etc... Remember to keep it updated.

29. Run special promotions and incentives

Make a contribution to a local charity's fundraiser by offering some free errand hours as a door prize. Perhaps contact
your local "welcome wagon" and add a gift certificate to
their package. A tip: always attach a list of services to the
gift certificate so that they know what they can use it for.

30. Community Leadership

This idea takes some time and can't be rushed. Donate
some of your free time to a non-profit organization that
interests you. Quite often you will be working side by side
with someone who might be influential in getting a referral
for you.

Some of these tips were provided with permission by Mr. Brian
Azar, the Sales Doctor. Mr. Azar is an international public
speaker, coach, author, and trainer and an advocate of lifelong
learning. Brian has been helping others to help themselves for
over 20 years. Through his work and research, he has devised
creative methods for transforming negative energy, lack of
motivation and poor communication skills into productive and
positive growth. He proves that self-realization and positive
motivation are the keys to success. He can be reached through
his website at www.salesdoctor.com.

Chapter 15
The Media

It is an excellent idea to send out a press release to all the local media agencies once you have your new concierge service department established. A truly GREAT way to get some free advertising!

I have included two press releases that were sent out about my own company during various times in the last few years. The second one is obviously the most recent. Both releases have gotten us newspaper articles and interviews in varying degrees.

SAMPLE PRESS RELEASE

For more information, contact:

Katharine C. Giovanni
Triangle Concierge, Inc.
919-852-5500; or visit our website at:
www.triangleconcierge.com

For immediate release:

Triangle Concierge, Inc. and Executive Staffing Group form alliance providing Triangle area companies with "corporate concierge services" as part of their benefits package.

Raleigh, July 27, 1999 : Triangle Concierge, Inc., the Triangle area's first corporate concierge service, and the Executive Staffing Group, which provides risk management, human resources, payroll and other services for small to mid-sized companies, have announced an alliance to bring corporate and lobby concierge services to Triangle companies.

Triangle Concierge was recently formed to offer both corporate and lobby concierge services to Triangle companies. The agreement will enable Executive Staffing to now offer concierge services as part of their complete human resource and employee benefit package. As good workers become increasingly hard to find in a hot U.S. economy, businesses are looking for new and effective ways to either attract or retain valuable employees. As a result, the concierge business is fast becoming the wave of the future, with concierge companies popping up in markets around the country.

According to Katharine Giovanni, President of Triangle Concierge: "Area companies will be able to offer employees a host of services — from picking up dry cleaning, running errands and managing catered business lunches to personal shopping, business referrals, ordering dinner and shopping for clothes."

"If you wish, we will buy your groceries, make your travel arrangements and arrange for a courier, " she noted. "Instead of making 20 calls, the employee has to make only one. Their concierges are equipped to help them manage some of those nagging 'to do's' in their life, and for people who have recently relocated to the triangle area, they can help eliminate all the wasted time looking for appropriate providers of various basic services.

The concierge idea has been around the hotel industry for some time and can be found in hotels around the world. Its transition from the hotel industry to the corporate world as part of an employee benefits package has been more recent. Over the past two years, the idea has begun to take hold, as companies located in cities such as Washington, Chicago and Boston have not only started to use corporate concierges, but are making them a part of their corporate benefit packages. Real estate management companies are also getting into the act, offering lobby concierge services to their tenants to add value to their properties and increase their marketability. Here in the Triangle, Triangle Concierge will place concierge services in office buildings to provide personal and business services to tenants.

Companies are increasingly using concierge services not only to attract and retain key employees, but also because they are reasoning that the less time people spend doing personal errands during the workday, the more time they can spend at their desks during the day and with their families at night. In other words, these services can increase both productivity and employee moral.

Changes in the U.S. workforce and an increasingly frenetic lifestyle for the family of the 90s has further fueled the trend towards use of corporate – and even personal — concierge services. According to a recent study of the U.S. work force released by the Families and Work Institute, the average worker spends

· 44 hours per week on the job
· 36 percent of workers say they often feel completely used up at the end of the workday.

And there is certainly no rest for us when we get home:

· 85% of workers have daily family responsibilities to go home to
· 78% of married workers have spouses who are also employed
· Weekends are consumed by errands and housekeeping
· 70% of all parents feel they don't spend enough time with their children.

"Looking at these statistics, it's easy to see why time has become a precious commodity in the '90s," said Ms. Giovanni. "The popularity of concierge services stems from the fact that people are stressed out, overworked, and need help dealing with life. We believe such a service will be especially useful in an area like the Triangle where we're seeing such a large influx of 'transplants'. Increasingly busy people want to spend what time they have with their families and nurturing themselves. They don't want to be forced to run errands. We're pleased to help bring this new national trend to companies and employees in the Triangle."

SAMPLE PRESS RELEASE

The following press release was written by Rebecca Antonelli at www.trianglePR.com

For immediate release:

Finding a Niche sometimes takes years, but it's worth the effort.

Reis & Trout – two fabulously famous brand marketers have been preaching the wonders of niche marketing for years. They say it's far easier to create your own focus, your own marketing "category" than try to compete in one that's already been established. For example, Coca-Cola came first – Pepsi will never capture first place – but – by creating a "new" category, 7up has managed to be number 1 in the "uncola" market. There are hundreds of examples of this nationally – and quite a few locally.

Here's how a few local entrepreneurs, a consultant, a public relations specialist and a club owner have found and captured their niche.

Katharine Giovanni with Triangle Concierge, Inc. created a local concierge service targeting corporate clients. At the time, she was one of the very few located in the Triangle. But she was not first. She was first, however, in creating a website for her company: www.triangleconcierge.com. What happened next should be an example to all of us. People from around the world started contacting Katharine to get information on how she operated her business and get tips on how to start and operate their own concierge business. While on the phone with one caller, her husband asked – "Are you doing that for free?" The answer was yes – and the light bulb turned on.

Within months, Giovanni had closed her local concierge business and started concentrating on building her consulting business. This included writing a book on how to start a concierge business and marketing herself as a speaker and consultant to trade journals and corporate organizations. "Today, I've consulted companies all over the world, Australia, England – and now I am being asked to help corporations start their own in-house concierge departments" says Giovanni, "I still get to help people, but now I'm one of only two companies in the world that do what I do, that I know of, instead of being one of the over 200 concierge companies in the United States. Medical and legal professionals have been specializing for years – I have decided to do the same thing, and it's working."

Rebecca Antonelli, founder of trianglepr.com has learned the same lesson. But, instead of it taking a year and a half, it took her over twelve. She started with a local marketing, advertising and public relations agency, Antonelli & associates. But as the Triangle began to change and grow, it was more and more difficult to predict the effectiveness of traditional advertising. She continued offering advertising creation, design and placement to her clients until one day she realized that she didn't want to do it anymore. She didn't love it. "If you don't love something, you're not going to succeed at it. I owed more to my clients than that," says Antonelli.

There was, however, one piece of her business she did love and always seemed to work: public relations. There, in black and white, she and her clients could determine the success or failure of a public relations campaign. Antonelli had always enjoyed helping small businesses grow, but they typically couldn't afford her fees, so she created a way that small and medium sized businesses could have an effective and efficient public relations program – without the high cost and high maintenance - by developing a website that facilitates the creation and distribution of press releases. She also continues her consulting, but instead of talking to one client at a time, she holds monthly "Meet the Media" events that teach attendees how to develop and encourage publicity for their companies.

Today, with over 100 members, trianglepr.com is fast becoming "the source for small business information" in the Triangle.

Chris Bender, owner of WickedSmile has transformed his business many times over in the past four years. Today, what started as an upscale eatery has become a haven for partygoers from all over the Triangle. The masterful mix of reggae-pop-hip music, funky décor and late night hours attracts club-goers in numbers he couldn't touch when his business was a traditional restaurant. WickedSmile is in a league of it's own. Bender's response to the success of his focus is amazingly nonchalant "I want to use my business to give people what they want. I just listen to people and make changes one at a time. Sometimes they're small, other times there huge. I don't find it scary, though. If you're not refining and changing and adapting, you're gonna get left behind."

The lesson to be learned from all these people is that constant monitoring of your business is a must. As Antonelli says, "When you find where you need to be, what you should be doing, the rest will take care of itself."

Chapter 16
Bibliography

The following books and webpages provided me with some great information and are wonderful resources.

1. <u>Zig Ziglar's Secrets of Closing the Sale</u>, Zig Ziglar, Berkley Books, New York 1984.

2. <u>The Contract and Fee-Setting Guide for Consultants and Professionals</u>, Howard L. Shenson, John Wiley & Sons, Inc., New York 1990.

3. <u>Selling your Services to the Meetings Market</u>, Bill Quain, Ph.D., Meeting Professionals International, 1993.

4. <u>The Meeting Planner's Guide to Logistics and Arrangements</u>, Stanley Mark Wolfson, Institute for Meeting and Conference Management, Washington DC, 1986.

5. Entrepreneur Magazine's "Concierge Services", http://www.entrepreneurmag.com/entmag/hotbiz99/concierge.html

6. Entrepreneur Magazine's "Personal Concierge Services", http://www.entrepreneurmag.com/startup/topbiz99/personal.html

7. Entrepreneur Magazine's "Senior Concierge Services", http://www.entrepreneurmag.com/startups/bsu_top10.hts

8. Entrepreneur Magazine's "Now Serving", http://www.entrepreneurmag.com/page.hts?N=6805

9. Entrepreneur Magazine's "Consider it Done", http://www.entrepreneurmag.com/page.hts?N=5383

10. http://www.errandinfo.com

Chapter 17
Helpful Books and Websites

Budgeting:

1. 9 Steps to Financial Freedom by Suze Orman, Crown Pub., 1997

2. 10 Minute Guide to Household Budgeting (10 Minute Guides) by Tracey Longo, IDG Books Worldwide, 1997

3. Bonnie's Household Budget Book : The Essential Workbook for Getting Control of Your Money by Bonnie Runyan McCullough, St. Martin's Press, 1996

4. How to Survive without your Salary by Charles Long, Warwick Pub., 1996

5. The Budget Kit : The Common Cents Money Management Workbook by Judy Lawrence, Dearborn Trade, 1997

6. The Courage to be Rich: Creating a Life of Material and Spiritual Abundance by Suze Orman, Riverhead Books, 1999

7. Some helpful websites include: www.homebudgeting.com and www.stretcher.com

Meeting/Event Planning:

1. Event Planning : The Ultimate Guide to Successful Meetings, Corporate Events, Fundraising Galas, Conferences, Conventions, and Other Special functions by Judy Allen, John Wiley & Sons, 1999

2. Planning Successful Meetings and Events : A Take-Charge Assistant Book by Ann J. Boehme, Amacom, 1998

3. Selling your Services to the Meetings Market By Bill Quain, Ph.D. Meeting Professionals International, 1993.

4. The Meeting Planner's Guide to Logistics and Arrangements by Stanley Mark Wolfson, Institute for Meeting and Conference Management, Washington DC, 1986.

5. Meeting Professionals International at www.mpiweb.org

Brochure Design:

1. Fresh Ideas in Brochure Design by Terri Alekzander, North Light Books, 1997

2. The Independent Consultant's Brochure and Letter Handbook by Herman Holtz, John Wiley & Sons, 1995

Business Plans:

1. The Complete Book of Business Plans : Simple Steps to Writing a Powerful Business Plan by Joseph A. Covello and Brian J. Hazelgren, Sourcebooks Trade, 1994

2. Some helpful websites include:
   www.bplans.com
   www.planware.org/busplan.htm

Starting your own Business

1. Small Business Start up Guide: A Surefire Blueprint to Succesfully Launch your own Business by Hal Root and Steve Koenig, Sourcebooks Trade, 1997

2. The Complete Idiot's Guide to Starting Your Own Business by Ed Paulsonack, MacMillan General Reference, 1998

3. Some helpful websites include:
   www.sba.org (the Small Business Administration)
   www.geocities.com/wallstreet/2172
   www.villagesoft.com/msprods/solution.htm.

Sales and Marketing:

1. <u>Knock your Socks off Selling</u> by Jeffrey Gitomer and Ron Zemke, Amacom, 1999

2. <u>Marketing for Dummies</u> by Alexander Hiam, IDG Books Worldwide, 1997

3. <u>Zig Ziglar's Secrets of Closing the Sale</u> by Zig Ziglar, Berkley Books, New York 1984.

4. Mr. Brian Azar, The Sales Catalyst, <u>www.salesdoctor.com</u>

Contracts:

1. <u>The Contract and Fee-Setting Guide for Consultants and Professionals</u> by Howard L. Shenson, John Wiley & Sons, Inc., New York 1990.

Creating your own Website:

1. <u>Creating Webpages for Dummies, 4th Edition</u> by Bud E. Smith and Arthur Bebak, IDG Books Worldwide, 1998

The Concierge Industry:

1. **The International Concierge and Errand Association.** For more information, you may contact them via email at carlam@bellatlantic.net

Experience

"Experience is a matter of sensibility and intuition, of seeing and hearing the significant things, of paying attention at the right moments, of understanding and coordinating. Experience is not what happens to a man; it is what a man does with what happens to him."

Aldous Huxley (1894–1963)

Chapter 18

Sample Forms and Applications

On the next few pages you will find some helpful forms and applications that many of my clients have used. As I've said before, there are almost 10,000 ways to do this, these forms are merely an example of one.

Also included is a very simple business plan for you to use as a guide when you create your own.

Lastly, a sample employee handbook has been added for you to use when your company grows to the point of actually hiring employees.

Good luck!

Sample Employment Application

(For employees without a resume)

Personal Information

First Name:_____

Middle Initial: _____

Last Name: _____

Address:_____

City, State, Zip Code: _____

Home Telephone: (   ) _____

Work Telephone: (   ) _____

E-mail Address:_____

Social Security Number: _____

Date of Birth: _____

Date of availability for employment: _____

Have you ever been arrested?   (   ) yes (   ) no

If yes, please explain:

_____

_____

Education

1. Name and address of School, Business School,

College/University: _____

   Years attended: _____

   Degree: _____

2. Name and address of School, Business School,
College/University: _____
    Years attended: _____
    Degree: _____

3. Name and address of School, Business School,
College/University: _____
    Years attended: _____
    Degree: _____

Special Training:

Please include Military, Certificates, Specific Courses, Correspondence Schools, Adult Education, etc.

  1. School or Agency: _____
      Subject: _____
      Length of Training: _____

  2. School or Agency: _____
      Subject: _____
      Length of Training: _____

  3. School or Agency: _____
      Subject: _____
      Length of Training: _____

Work Experience:

May we contact your present employer? (   ) yes   (   ) no

1.   Employed from (month/year): _____ to _____
Name of Employer: _____
Supervisor's Name: _____
Address: _____
City/State/Zip Code: _____
Telephone Number: (   ) _____
Job Title: _____
Job Duties: (continue on separate paper if necessary)

_____

_____

_____

Reason for Leaving: (continue on separate paper if necessary)

_____

_____

\2.   Employed from (month/year): _____ to _____
Name of Employer: _____
Supervisor's Name: _____
Address: _____
City/State/Zip Code: _____
Telephone Number: (   ) _____
Job Title: _____

Job Duties: (continue on separate paper if necessary)

_____

_____

_____

Reason for Leaving: (continue on separate paper if necessary)

_____

_____

3.   Employed from (month/year): _____ to _____

Name of Employer: _____

Supervisor's Name: _____

Address: _____

City/State/Zip Code: _____

Telephone Number: (   ) _____

Job Title: _____

Job Duties: (continue on separate paper if necessary)

_____

_____

_____

Reason for Leaving: (continue on separate paper if necessary)

_____

_____

Thank you

Sample Membership Application

(Should be printed on your own letterhead)

First Name: _____

Middle Initial: _____

Last Name: _____

Suffix: _____

Nickname: _____

Organization Name: _____

Title: _____

Department: _____

Address: _____

City _____

State _____

Zip Code: _____

Work Phone number: (   ) _____

Fax number: (   ) _____

E-mail Address: _____

Home Address: _____

City _____

State _____

Zip Code: _____

Home Telephone: (   ) _____

Personal Information:

Date of Birth: _____
Your Interests: _____
Marital Status: ( ) single   ( ) married

Spouse

First Name: _____
Last Name: _____
Date of Birth: _____
Interests: _____

Children

Name: _____
      Date of Birth: _____
Name: _____
      Date of Birth: _____
Name: _____
      Date of Birth: _____
Interrests: _____

Payment Information: Please Check One

☐   Check
☐   Credit Card
☐   Concierge Account

Thank you!

Sample Vendor Application

BUSINESS CATEGORY: _____

CONTACT NAME: _____

TITLE: _____

COMPANY: _____

ADDRESS: _____

CITY, STATE, ZIP CODE: _____

TELEPHONE: ( ) _____

FAX: ( ) _____

E-MAIL:
_____

WEBPAGE:
_____

DESCRIPTION OF SERVICES:

_____
_____
_____
_____

REFERENCES:

Please give us the names of three clients (either current or within the past six months).

Name: _____

Address: _____

Telephone Number: (   ) _____

Name: _____

Address: _____

Telephone Number: (   ) _____

Name: _____

Address: _____

Telephone Number: (   ) _____

Please attach your company brochure and business card so that we may add it to your file.

THANK YOU!

Reprinted with the permission of Go-Fers Unlimited

®GO-FERS UNLIMITED, INC.™

1823 Ashland Avenue ■ Evanston, Illinois 60201
Ph (847) 866-8000 Fax (847) 866-8552
Website: www.wegoferu.com
Email: wegoferu@aol.com

Date_____ Time_____ Invoice#_____

Requested by: _____

Phone: _____Fax: _____

Method of payment

Cash   Check   Credit card   Account   Purchase Order # _____

| VISA | MC | Discover |

Card number: Expiration date:_____

Time out: _____ Cost: $_____ Extended: $ _____Total: $_____

Bill to: _____

_____

Deliver to: _____

Details of Request:

Please find receipts attached

193

Reprinted with the permission of Go-Fers Unlimited

GO-FERS UNLIMITED, INC.™

1823 Ashland Avenue ▪ Evanston, Illinois 60201
Ph (847) 866-8000 Fax (847) 866-8552 ▪ Website: www.wegoferu.com ▪ Email: wegoferu@aol.com

Daily Records of Runs

A Professional Errand Service

Date_____   Starting mileage_____   Gas $_____

Requestor	Kind of Errand	Time In / Time Out	Cost $
_____	_____	_____ / _____	_____
_____	_____	_____ / _____	_____
_____	_____	_____ / _____	_____
_____	_____	_____ / _____	_____
_____	_____	_____ / _____	_____
_____	_____	_____ / _____	_____
_____	_____	_____ / _____	_____
_____	_____	_____ / _____	_____
_____	_____	_____ / _____	_____
_____	_____	_____ / _____	_____
_____	_____	_____ / _____	_____

Notes:

Total extended reimbursements: $_____ Today's Collections: $_____

Ending Mileage: _____

Sample Driver Trip Sheet

There are 10,000 ways to set this up, this is merely a sample of one.

Name:_____   Date: _____

Starting Mileage: _____   Starting Time: _____

Ending Mileage: _____   Ending Time: _____

Name of Store/Address of Home	Client Name	Arrival Time	Depart Time	Total $

Notes:

Sample Errand Order Sheet

There are 10,000 ways to set this up, this is merely a
sample of one.

Today's Date: _____

Client ID #: _____

 Name: _____

Company Name: _____

Pick up from:　　　(　) Home　(　) Office

Street Address: _____

Directions: _____

_____

_____

_____

Delivery to: (　) Home　(　) Office

Street Address: _____

Directions: _____

_____

_____

_____

Payment via: (   ) Check   (   ) Visa   (   ) Mastercard

Credit Card Number: _____

Expiration Date: _____

Errands Needed Done:

1.

2.

3.

4.

5.

6.

7.

8.

9.

10.

Customers signature required upon receipt

Sample Daily Dry Cleaning Trip Sheet

If you don't want to outsource to a dry cleaner who delivers and prefer to do it yourself in-house, then this form might help you.

DATE: _____

Client Name	Pick up Address	Store Location	Date Ready	Time Delivered	Total $

Notes:

Reprinted with the permission of Go-Fers Unlimited

GO-FERS UNLIMITED INCORPORATED
Services Currently Offered

Personal/Professional Errands

- Run errands large or small
- Writing letters and meaningful thank-you cards
- Deliver packages and documents
- Post office needs
- Visit the hospitalized and deliver clothes, magazines and flowers
- Pick up movie or theater tickets
- Dry cleaning- pick up/drop off
- Child care finders
- Personal shopper or gift returns
- Gift-wrapping
- Shoe repair
- Video rentals and/or returns
- Motor Vehicle Services
- "Got a gripe service" for difficult to handle people or situations
- Have keys made
- New move unpacking
- Wait for the service man

Business/Executive Services

- Concierge services
- Meeting coordination
- Telephone services
- Internet research
- Office supplies
- Banking services
- Printing services
- Notary service
- File legal documents
- Picking up airline tickets
- Film drop-off and delivery
- Making travel arrangements
- Address and mail seasonal greeting cards
- Pick up building supplies
- Blueprints & Architectural drawings
- We'll even take your dog or cat to the veterinarian or groomer
- Wait for delivery or serviceman, verify workmanship, sign off and lock up your home
- We'll find the perfect gift for your valued Client, Employee or Boss
- Gift returns
- Hunt for new house or apartment

Your Company is considering offering a concierge service to it's employees and would like to know if this type of service would be of value to you. Please take a moment to let us know what you think!

What is a concierge service?

A concierge service is a service to assist you with *personal* or *professional* errands. Someone to take care of that endless to-do list or run those time consuming errands that you really don't have time to take care of after business hours. Our services are unlimited! (please refer to our list on your left)

Would you use this type of service? ___Yes ___No

If so, how often do you think you would call for errand assistance?

____not at all ____once a month ____once a week ____more often

What types of errands do you need handled ?(pick 3)_____

_____

Are there any services not listed that you would like to see offered? ____Yes ____No If you answered yes, please tell us what they are.

_____

Would you be inclined to call for a parent or a spouses needs? ____Yes ____No

Please be honest, how much would you expect to pay for this type of time-saver? $_____.00 / per hour

Do you think that a service like this would be beneficial to you? ____Yes ____No

Do you think that you would be more focused at work if you didn't have to worry about all the tasks you had to take care of after work? ____Yes ____No

Would you like to see this type of service offered as part of a benefits package? ____Yes ____No

We want to know how *you* feel, please feel free to write down any other comments you may have!

_____

_____

_____

_____

_____

Thank you for taking the time to tell us what you think! We really do know how valuable your time is! We look forward to serving you in the future!

GO-FERS UNLIMITED, INCORPORATED is sensitive to the needs of the humanity, 10% of all proceeds go back to the community it serves. TM

Sample Brochure

Does this sound familiar?

Not only do you work full time and have a family, but you also have to do the following (after fighting rush hour traffic).

- Pick-up the dry cleaning, groceries and the kids.

- Send flowers to someone.

- Call the travel agent to arrange a vacation or surf the web looking for one.

- Call the carpet cleaner.

- Get some tickets for an event you want to go to.

- Arrange a party for your neighborhood, office or family.

- Clean your house because you're having company this weekend.

- Pay this month's bills.

- Finally get to that work you brought home from the office.

Before you call the people who will cart you off to that nice rubber room you've been dreaming about, we would like you to call us. We all lead busy lives and there never seems to be enough time to do everything. Triangle Concierge can help you by taking some of the "to do" items off of your list.

Don't Delay
Call Us Now!

Call us today so that we can do the things that need to be done, and you can do the things that you want to do - like spending more time with your family. **With our help you can really DO IT ALL!**

VISIT OUR WEBSITE!

www.triangleconcierge.com

Triangle Concierge, Inc.
7410 Chapel Hill Road
Raleigh, NC 27607
Tel: 919-852-5500
Fax: 919-852-5515
E-Mail:
kgiovanni@triangleconcierge.com

Spend
more time
doing things
you actually
want to do
and
less time
doing the
things you
have to!

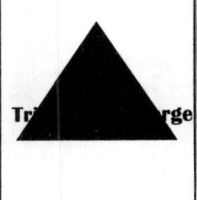

Summary

The concierge idea has been around the hotel industry for some time and can be found in hotels around the world. Recently, however, it has begun to emerge in the corporate world. Many companies located in cities such as Washington, Chicago and Boston have not only started to use corporate concierges but are making them a part of their corporate benefit packages. Other companies are offering concierge services to their employees as an optional payroll deduction.

Triangle Concierge Inc. is both a personal assistant and a meeting/event/travel planner. We give some valuable time back to busy professionals. Rather than spend part of their busy workday ordering flowers, planning a vacation, checking airfare/transportation, ordering tickets or leaving early to pick up dry cleaning they can just call us to do these tasks for them.

Many businesses are turning to companies like Triangle Concierge in order to keep their employees from spending too much time conducting personal business while at the office. Show your employees how valuable they really are to you! Give your employees the gift of time and allow them to concentrate better during the day while spending more time with their families at night.

Our Services

Triangle Concierge is designed to make your life a little bit easier by taking away a great many of those pesky "to do" items that we all have to deal with every day. We are dedicated to alleviating some of the stress that you are under and giving you back some time to do other more important things ... like spending time with your family, taking a walk, going to the health club or going out to dinner with friends!

Would you like to go on a special night out?
   Tickets - sports events/theatre/concerts
   Dinner recommendations/reservations
   Transportation needs

Planning A Special Event?
   Florists, photographers
   Musicians, entertainers

Need help planning a meeting, conference or seminar?
   Meeting Planning
   VIP arrangements

Would you like to go on vacation? How about a special weekend away? Golf?
   Travel, Vacations
   Tee times

Relocating? Need some help at the office?
   Relocation Services
   Business Referrals
   Business Support

Too many errands to do? Need a gift? Need some cards or invitations adressed and sent?
   Errand Service
   Gift and Card Assistance

Not only can Clients access our Business Referral Service, but we can send our staff to wait for the service vendors while you're at work!

Maids and Cleaning Professionals,
Mechanics,
Plumbers,
Electricians,
Realtors,
Builders,
Architects,
Childcare
Pet Care,
Landscapers,
Carpet Cleaners
Locksmiths,
Painters and Wallpaper Hangers,
Health and Fitness Clubs,
Moving Companies and more!

Membership Information

Corporate, Individual and Express Memberships are available.

Meeting/Event Planning, Errand/House Sitting Services and Card/Gift Services are all subject to additional fees.

Errand/HouseSitting Service requires 24 hours advance notice for requests. Emergency requests will always be accommodated whenever we can.

Call Now!

Sample Brochure

According to USA Today:

"Companies and Associations are so over-burdened with meetings that experts say it's a wonder any work gets done."

... let us give you back some time by allowing us to do some of your work for you.

F or more information about our services please call or write us at:

Meeting Planning Plus, Inc.
7410 Chapel Hill Road
Raleigh, NC 27607
Tel: 919-852-5500
Fax: 919-852-5515

Or you can e-mail us at:
kgiovanni@meetingplanningplus.com

Come Visit us on the Web!

www.meetingplanningplus.com
www.citysearch.com/rdu/mppinc

MPP's mission is to provide the utmost in customer service. We are dedicated to the complete satisfaction of both our customers and their attendees.

Meeting
Planning
Plus, Inc.

Your
Meeting
Specialists!

Experience

Experience is the number one reason to use MPP as there's less risk that something will go wrong. MPP develops contacts on a continuing basis which helps us give our clients the best the industry has to offer.

We have over 26 years of combined experience in meeting planning, sales, marketing and customer relations.

We are members of the Raleigh, Durham and Morrisville Chambers of Commerce, The Sports Council and Meeting Professionals International.

Productivity

Productivity is another reason to use MPP. The amount of hours that it will take us to produce your meeting is valuable time. Time that you are being given back to do other equally valuable work. It is freeing up your staff to do other valuable work that wouldn't otherwise get done.

MPP can either do the entire meeting, increasing the productivity of the client's staff, or just a part of the event. This leaves the client's staff the time to organize the rest of the meeting and everyone is a winner!

MPP is completely customer focused and will help you and your attendees obtain a **return on your investment (ROI)** by finding out what each of your goals are and assisting you in attaining those goals.

Our Services

Contract Negotiations
Logistics
Exhibits
Banquets
Entertainment
Audio Visual
Speaker Signs
Speaker
   Coordination
Site Selection
Site Management
Travel Arrangements
Hotel Negotiations
Spouse Programs
Children's Programs
Continuing Education
   Coordination
Food and Beverage
Attendee Eveluations
Post-Meeting Follow-up

Registration Services Include:
Pre-registration, on-site registration and on-site management.

Sample Concierge Company

Employee Handbook

Sample Concierge Company

123 Sample Lane, Sample City, USA
Tel: 555-555-5555 Fax: 555-555-5556
Website: www.sampleconcierge.com

Dear Sample Concierge Staff:

As employees of Sample Concierge, it is important that each of you be aware of our current policies and procedures. This handbook contains easily referenced guidelines that pertain to employment policies, benefits and general information that each of you will find useful while working here.

It is our firm policy that family comes first and we will always do our best to accommodate any reasonable situation that may come up with our employees and their families.

Please remember that my door is always open for anyone who wishes to talk to me about their job, our policies, recommend changes, or ask questions of any kind.

I'm looking forward to working with you.

Sincerely,

Joseph Van Pelt
President

Table of Contents

The Corporate Policies that follow contain policies adopted by Sample Concierge, Inc. All employees of Sample Concierge, Inc. are required to adhere to the requirements of these Corporate Policies. While Department policies may provide additional requirements for their employees; such policies must be consistent with and meet the requirements of the applicable Corporate Policy.

Employment Policies
> Equal Opportunity Policy/Affirmative Action
>> Compliance
> Statement
> Drug-Free Workplace Statement
> Conflict of Interest
> Incident Policy
> Sexual Harassment
> Smoking
> Substance Abuse
> Infectious Disease Policy

Annual Performance Evaluation Form

Employee Benefits

1. *Social Security* - all employees shall participate in the social security program

2. *Workman's Compensation* - All employees shall be covered by Workman's Compensation Insurance.

3. *Unemployment Compensation* - All employees shall be covered by state and federal employment security laws.

4. *Medical/Dental/Disability Insurance* - All full-time employees shall be entitled to an individual medical/dental/disability insurance plan starting in 30 days or at next available start date. Employees may be required to pay a portion of their premium depending on their plan selection. New employees may be subjected to pre-existing conditions depending on insurance company policies.

5. All employees shall be eligible to participate in the 401(k) Plan. Participation is voluntary and employees are eligible to enroll in the Plan upon date of hire.

Holidays

Sample Concierge will be closed on the following holidays
(except for special events):

New Year's Day, January 1
Memorial Day
Independence Day, July 4
Labor Day
Thanksgiving for 2 days
Christmas Eve Day, December 24
Christmas Day, December 25
2 floating holidays

Vacation Leave

Full-time employees shall be granted vacation based on their
years of service with the company. The following schedule will
determine the amount of leave an employee is entitled to.

After 6 months employment, employee will receive 2 days of
vacation leave. This time, however, cannot be taken congru-
ently without approval of management and cannot be carried
over to the next year.

1 year	1 week
2 - 4 years	2 weeks
5 - 9 years	3 weeks
10 or more	4 weeks

Regardless of the amount of vacation employees are entitled to, employees may carry forward up to one (1) week of vacation into the following year with their supervisors' permission.

Upon retirement or termination of employment, any unused annual leave accrued shall be paid to the employee in a lump sum payment.

Personal Leave

Regular full-time employees are eligible for personal leave. Personal leave can be used when a member of the employee's immediate family requires his/her attention, when there is an emergency that only the employee can handle, bereavements not covered under funeral leave (subject to approval by Management) etc. Personal leave hours may not be carried over from one year to the next. Personal leave is not vacation leave and therefore is not intended to supplement vacation periods. Management's approval is required for personal leave hours to be used.

Personal leave shall be charged against sick leave and may not be granted in excess of accumulated sick leave. The number of hours granted would be governed by the circumstances of the case, but in no event shall they exceed 40 hours in any calendar year. Requested personal leave in excess of 40 hours in any calendar year will be charged to vacation leave until the vacation leave balance is depleted and then to leave without pay.

Military Leave

All employees who are officers or enlisted in any component of the armed forces of the United States shall, when ordered by the proper authority to active duty or service, be entitled to a leave of absence for such active service. There will be no loss of status. There will be no loss of pay for up to 20 working days per calendar year.

Sick Leave

Each employee shall receive 6 days sick leave yearly with pay after 1 year of employment. New employees will receive 3 sick days after 6 months of employment with no days taken off. Employee shall carry over a maximum of one year's worth of sick days over to the next year.

Employees must notify their supervisor each day the employee is unable to work. While the company will pay for authorized sick days, employees are expected to be honest in requesting and using sick leave. Employees suspected of abusing their sick leave benefit may be required to bring a doctor statement for any sick leave used.

Under no circumstances should an employee claim sick leave benefits to work on another job and any abuse of this benefit will be taken into account during performance evaluations. Appropriate disciplinary action will be taken if sick leave abuse is discovered, not to exclude termination.

Funeral Leave

The purpose of funeral leave is to provide regular full-time employees with the time to attend funerals of immediate family members and to handle related affairs without disrupting income. The maximum amount of funeral leave granted for bereavement will be determined by the relationship of the employee to the deceased as listed below:

1. Each full-time employee is allowed to use up to three (3) days for deaths in the immediate family. This includes spouse, children, mother, father or sibling of the employee, grandparents, mother-in-law, father-in-law, siblings-in-law, stepparent, stepsiblings, grandparents-in-law and grand-child.
2. Each full-time employees may be granted time off from work without loss of regular pay or deductions from leave balances for attending the funeral of a relative not a

member of their immediate family but not to exceed 1 work day (8 hours). This includes uncles, aunts, nieces, nephews, first generation cousins, and in-laws not defined in the above paragraph.

Maternity Leave

Sample Concierge is in compliance with the Family and Medical Leave Act of 1993. It is the policy of the company to grant an employee up to a maximum of 12 weeks of unpaid leave in any 12 month period to care for a newborn or newly adopted child, a seriously ill family member or for the employee's own serious illness. Accumulated sick leave and vacation time may be used during maternity leave.

Administrative Leave

Employees will be placed on administrative leave with pay if summoned to serve jury duty. Administrative leave for jury duty will not be charged against the employee's annual vacation, sick leave or personal leave and the employee will be entitled to any juror's pay.

Due to a subpoena as a witness (except as plaintiff or defendant) an employee will be granted administrative leave with pay.

Workweek

Sample Concierge is open from Monday through Friday. Hours will vary. Employees are allowed 1/2 to 1 hour for lunch and regular morning/afternoon breaks. Workweek will consist of 35 to 40 hours. Overtime starts after 40 hours.

Time and Attendance

A formal record of the employee's time and attendance will be maintained.

Outside Employment

A person who accepts full-time employment with Sample Concierge assumes a primary professional obligation to the company. Any other employment or enterprise in which the employee engages for income must be understood to be secondary to his work at the company. Employees may not re-arrange schedules to accommodate outside employment. Outside employment must not be a conflict of interest or have the perception of being a conflict of interest with his/her company work.

Employee will not sell or arrange any personal arrangements or business while working on company premises or while on company time.

If outside employment becomes a problem for the employee to perform his/her company work the employee will be asked to correct the problem, not to exclude the termination of the outside employment. Any employee working outside the company on a regular basis should inform his/her supervisor.

Increases in Salary

After 12 months of service and a yearly performance evaluation, employees will be eligible for advancement to a higher salary upon recommendation of the employee's immediate supervisor and upon the concurrence of the President. Annual cost-of-living increases will be granted as deemed appropriate by the management. A performance evaluation will be conducted every six months.

Pay Day - All salaried employees will be paid twice a month.

Termination Process

Although an employee may terminate their employment at will, the company requests an employee to give at least 2 weeks notice via a letter of resignation submitted to their immediate supervisor. The salary of an employee whose services are terminated before the end of the month will be prorated on the basis of workdays during the month of termination. There will be no payment for any unused accrued sick leave or vacation leave at time of termination.

Employment Policies

Equal Opportunity Policy/Affirmative Action Compliance Statement

The President and employees of Sample Concierge reaffirm the following policy:

In compliance with Title VI and Title VII of the Civil Rights Act of 1964, Executive Order 11246 as amended, Title IX of the Education Amendments of 1972, Sections 503 and 504 of the Rehabilitation Act of 1973, the Americans With Disabilities Act of 1990, the Family & Medical Leave Act of 199, the Civil Rights Act of 1991 and other federal rules and regulations, Sample Concierge does not discriminate on the basis of race, color, religion, gender, age, national origin, physical challenge, visual or hearing impairment, disability or status as a veteran.

Drug-Free Workplace Policy Statement

Sample Concierge, in compliance with the Drug-Free Workplace Act of 1988, hereby gives notice to all its employees that the statements listed below constitute the company's formal policy. It is in the best interests of both the Company and its employees to provide education, awareness, and assistance where appropriate relative to the dangers inherent in the unlawful manufacture, distribution, dispensation, possession or use of a controlled substance in the workplace. The special consequences of drug abuse in the workplace include the threatened safety to co-workers by those who are impaired by drugs the increased danger of defective or substandard services being provided to the public and diminished productivity.

1. The unlawful manufacture, distribution, dispensation, possession or use of a controlled substance in any company work area, or outside of company when on company time is prohibited.

2. As a condition of employment, employees must abide by the terms of this policy.

3. Any employee who is convicted of any state or federal criminal drug statue for drug-related misconduct in the workplace must report the conviction within five (5) working days to the President.

4. Violations will result in administrative sanctions, ranging in severity from formal counseling to termination of employment, immediately or within 30 days, whether or not the violation results in conviction under state and federal criminal drug statues for misconduct in the workplace. Satisfactory participation in a company approved drug abuse assistance or rehabilitation program may be required as a condition of continued employment by the company of all employees who violate this prohibition and are not terminated from employment.

Conflict of Interest

An employee has an obligation and responsibility to report to their immediate supervisor any outside business or financial activity which is or may be in conflict with the interests of Sample Concierge or which interferes with the performance of his/her duties. Violations of this policy will be considered grounds for disciplinary action, up to and including termination.

No employee shall conduct outside business or financial activity during business hours when employee is working for Sample Concierge.

Incident Policy

Sample Concierge is committed to maintaining a workplace environment that is safe and secure for all employees of the company. Threats, threatening behavior, acts of violence and unwanted attention directed against other employees, visitors, or guests by anyone will not be tolerated.

Sexual Harassment

Sample Concierge condemns sexual harassment in any form and is committed to providing a safe environment free of it for everyone. Sexual harassment means unwelcome sexual advances, requests for sexual favors and other verbal or physical conduct of a sexual nature.

All complaints concerning sexual harassment will be thoroughly investigated, with care taken to protect the rights of the
complainant as well as the rights of the alleged harasser. A
finding of sexual harassment will result in appropriate disciplinary action, which may include a range of actions up to, and
including dismissal. Legal actions may be taken.

Smoking

Smoking and the use of all tobacco products are prohibited in
the office and in the lobby concierge set-ups.

Substance Abuse

Sample Concierge strives to ensure that all employees are
provided with a supportive work environment. Therefore, the
company will provide reasonable assistance for employees in
dealing with personal problems such as substance abuse,
including alcohol and drug abuse.

SAMPLE

PERFORMANCE EVALUATION

Employee Name: _____

Title: _____

Rating Period: From: _____ To: _____

Review Date: _____

Mid-year Review Date: _____

Procedures:

1. Supervisor identifies major skills required for job success, lists them and communicates these to employees at beginning of appraisal cycle.
2. Employee completes the self-appraisal (parts I-II) before scheduled appraisal meeting
3. Supervisor reviews employees self-appraisal and evaluates employees performance (parts I-IV)
4. Supervisor and employee meet for the appraisal interview to discuss their ratings, sign the evaluation form and make comments.
5. Form is reviewed and signed by the President.

Part I - Skills

The following is a list of skills which apply to this position

Skills	Not Acceptable		Partially Achieving Expectations		Achieving Expectations		Exceed Expecta
	Emp	Supv	Emp	Supv	Emp	Supv	Emp

Notes:

Part II – Performance Standards

Skills	Not Acceptable		Partially Achieving Expectations		Achieving Expectations		Exceeding Expectations	
	Emp	Supv	Emp	Supv	Emp	Supv	Emp	Supv
Knowledge of Job: Understanding job procedures, equipment & responsibilities								
Quantity of Work: Completing tasks thoroughly and accurately								
Dependability: Reliability to do assigned work and meet deadlines and schedules								
Coordination of Work: planning and organizing of work, tasks and use of company resources								
Judgement: Decision making and problem solving ability								
Cooperation: Willingness to accept supervisory instructions and directions and willingness to apply effort								

Skills	Not Acceptable		Partially Achieving Expectations		Achieving Expectations		Exceeding Expectations	
	Emp	Supv	Emp	Supv	Emp	Supv	Emp	Supv
Interaction with Others: Willingness & ability to get along, interact and work with others, both internally and externally								
Initiative & Enthusiasm: Self-reliance and self-starting ability								
Commitment to Job: Demonstrating a consistent, dependable work effort, and a positive work attitude								
Attendance and Punctuality: using company time conscientiously								

Mid-year Discussion

Supervisor Comments:_____

_____

_____

_____

Employee Comments: _____

_____

_____

_____

Part III: Supervisor explains any rating from Part I or II that is "not acceptable". _____

_____

_____

Part IV: Overall Performance rating of employee

❏   Not Acceptable

❏   Partially Achieving Expectations

❏   Achieving Expectation

❏   Exceeding Expectations

224

Part V: Action Plans for Improving Performance in Present Position:

<u>Annual Review:</u>

Supervisor Comments: _____

_____

_____

_____

Employee Comments: _____

_____

_____

_____

_____ _____

Supervisor Signature   Date

_____ _____

Employee Signature   Date

Example of a Concierge Service

Business Plan

Confidentiality Agreement

The undersigned reader acknowledges that the information provided by John Smith in this business plan is confidential and; therefore, reader agrees not to disclose it without the express permission of John Smith.

It is acknowledged by reader that information to be furnished in this business plan is in all respects confidential in nature, other than information which is in the public domain through other means and that any disclosure or use of same by reader, may cause serious harm or damage to Sample Concierge.

Upon request, this document is to be immediately returned to John or Karen Smith.

_____   _____

Signature   Date

_____

Name (typed or printed)

This is a business plan. It does not imply offering of securities.

Introduction

John and Karen Smith started the Sample Concierge Company in January 1999 in Sample City and plans to open its doors by August 1999. Sample Concierge was recently formed to offer both corporate and lobby concierge services to area businesses who are now offering concierge services as part of their complete human resource and employee benefit packages. As good employees become increasingly hard to find in a hot U.S. economy, businesses are looking for new and effective ways to either attract or retain their valuable staff members. As a result, the concierge business is the wave of the future, with concierge companies popping up around the country.

Area companies will be able to offer employees a host of services that include: picking up dry cleaning, running errands, managing catered business lunches, personal shopping, business referrals, and ordering dinner to name a few. Sample Concierge can buy your groceries, make your travel arrangements and arrange for a courier. Now instead of making 20 calls, the employee only has to make one. Sample Concierge employees are equipped to help our clients manage some of those nagging 'to do's' in their life, and for people who have recently relocated to the area, our company can help eliminate all the wasted time looking for appropriate providers various basic services.

Mission Statement

Sample Concierge Company strives to offer outstanding service for busy executives in Sample City. Our mission is to place a concierge desk in the lobby of every office building in the greater Sample City area and to bring new meaning to the words "employee benefits package". We are dedicated to giving our clients some extra time by making concierge services a part of their corporate benefits package.

Companies are using concierge services to attract and retain key employees, as well as to increase productivity by keeping their employees at their desks during work hours. Using a concierge service benefits the employee by freeing up more time for them to enjoy doing the things they choose when the workday ends without the stress of running errands.

Changes in the U.S. workforce and an increasingly frenetic lifestyle for the family of the 90s has further fueled the trend towards use of corporate and even personal concierge services. According to a recent study of the U.S. work force released by the Families and Work Institute, the average worker spends:

- 44 hours per week on the job
- 36 percent of workers say they often feel completely used up at the end of the workday.

And there is certainly no rest for us when we get home:

- 85% of workers have daily family responsibilities to go home to
- 78% of married workers have spouses who are also employed
- Weekends are consumed by errands and housekeeping
- 70% of all parents feel they don't spend enough time with their children.

Looking at these statistics, it's easy to see why time has become a precious commodity in the '90s. The popularity of concierge services stems from the fact that people are stressed out, overworked, and need help dealing with life. Sample Concierge believes such a service will be especially useful in Sample City because there is such a large influx of transplants'. Increasingly busy people want to spend what time they have with their families and nurturing themselves. They don't want to be forced to run errands. We are pleased to help bring this new national trend to companies and employees in Sample City.

Unique Features

Sample Concierge is Sample City's premier corporate concierge service. It is designed to be the ultimate stress reliever by giving you back the one thing that you never have enough of -

time.

Let's use an example of someone's typical day. It is 5:00 p.m. and after a very long day at the office (where you still need to find a meeting planner, organize a sales trip for your boss, and get a computer consultant to come in) you have to fight rush hour traffic to get home. Once in your neighborhood you have to rush to the dry cleaners, buy groceries, pick up the kids and run home to cook dinner. After dinner you have to contact the travel agent, make dinner reservations for an upcoming outing with friends, send flowers to your sick aunt and arrange to have the carpet cleaned because your 3 year old spilled grape juice (all while being constantly interrupted by your kids).

Then your spouse reminds you that you need to plan a surprise birthday party for his mother for 50 people! Now you need a caterer, invitations and a cleaning company to come and clean your house! Oh... and don't forget you need to take a personal day tomorrow so that you can meet the washing machine repairman. Talk about stress! Not everyone has such a hectic schedule, but we all have days where we could certainly use more hours in the day (or at least a machine that could clone us so we could be in several places at once). Sample Concierge is a one-stop shop where you can send us your "to do" list and then consider it done. Instead of making hundreds of telephone calls both at the office and from home using up your valuable time, you just make one call, — to us.

Your time is valuable and Sample Concierge would like to give you some more of it so that you can spend more time with your family doing things that you actually want to do instead of the things that you have to do.

Marketing Objectives

Sample Concierge's marketing strategy starts with a website, www.sampleconcierge.com. that is currently on the Internet. Another website has been designed by CitySearch and will be up by the middle of March. Two "tiles" will be placed on several feature article pages for users to click on and locate our service. A synopsis of our company is located on the Sample City Chamber of Commerce's map project, and will be available to the public in March. In addition, a mailing will be sent out to various companies in the area announcing the business. Mailings will actually be sent out on a regular basis to market the service.

Furthermore, the Sample City Chapter of Meeting Professionals International is doing an article on Mrs. Smith that should be out towards the end of March. A press release will be sent out to all the local media agencies once the first corporate client is signed on and monthly thereafter. Concierge Services will be offered to area employees as part of a corporate benefit package or as a payroll deduction. Sample Concierge will set-up appointments with human resource

232

departments and corporate managers and will present our unique and professional services to them.

Additional and continuous marketing such as radio spots, magazine and newspaper advertisements will be considered as revenue increases.

Expected Accomplishments

Sample Concierge expects increased continuous revenue with profitability by the second year. The table (goals) shown below represents a five-year projection of the company's rate of growth.

Table 1

The numbers listed below are an example only and are not an actual representation

Description	Year 1	Year 2	Year 3	Year 4	Year 5
Gross Sales	$45,000	135,000	202,000	252,600	290,000
Growth Rate	—	300%	50%	25%	15%

Required Capital

In order for Sample Concierge to commence its operations, $115,000 will be needed. An investment of $20,000 will be required from each owner (numbers here are just samples). The owners of Sample Concierge will need to contribute $20,000 of their own funds and will require financing from a lender for an additional $75,000. The business requires a 3-year loan that will be repaid in monthly installments.

THE BUSINESS

Problem Statement

People have too much too do and not enough time in which to do it. That is today's basic problem. Sample Concierge aims to solve this problem by doing some of the everyday tasks for the client.

In today's market, companies and individuals do not have the time to do all the items they have on their "to do" list and still be able to spend some quality time with their families. Furthermore, if they need to plan a meeting or event they do not always have the time or the expertise to put it together on top of everything else they need to do. Shopping around for travel agents, caterers, florists, photographers, rental companies and musicians for an event takes a significant

234

amount of time. On top of everything else, it is hard to find the time to pick up/deliver dry cleaning, find courier services, solve computer problems, locate a particular type of restaurant and find a good service repairman.

Having an intermediary who has done the research for them and has established a relationship with these businesses can be invaluable. Customers actually have two choices. They can do everything themselves or they can hire someone to help them. The question then becomes how much you value your time. Sample Concierge can meet all your needs under the same roof. We are a one-stop shop so that our clients can make ONE phone call instead of hundreds thus saving them both time and money.

Description of the Business

Sample Concierge will do everything on a client's "to do" list for a reasonable yearly membership price. The partners intend to target area companies as its source of business. These companies will in turn offer concierge services to their employees as part of their corporate benefits packages. Sample Concierge has reliable and honest vendors available and have negotiated discounts with them for our clients.

Furthermore, each vendor promises to give Sample Concierge a 10% referral fee. This allows us to charge reasonable yearly membership rates. Our corporate office is open from 9:00 a.m to 5:00 p.m. Monday through Friday. We will offer our clients the following services:

Instead of running around during your lunch hour, fighting crowds on Saturday or racing around after 5 ... let us do your errands for you. We can pick up your dry cleaning, buy your groceries... whatever your needs are.

Sample Concierge can order all of your tickets for concerts, sporting events, holiday events, Broadway shows, or the ballet. We can arrange for your golf tee times, reserve a tennis court for you, arrange for you to go horseback riding or make a reservation for you to take a scuba diving lesson.

We can give you some dinner recommendations/reservations, arrange for a limousine, town car, bus, helicopter or charter plane. We can send flowers to that special someone for you, or can order arrangements for that special event. Let us help you find a DJ, band, magician, clown, comedian, impersonator or book a celebrity for your special event.

Sample Concierge can also help you with your Airline Reservations, Hotel/Motel Reservations, Ground Transportation, Vacation Rentals, Resort Recommendations/ Reservations, and Relocation Services. Plus we can assist your employees with their relocation! We can arrange for

Short Term Condo/Apartment Rentals, Airlines and rental car reservations, Movers and Storage.

Clients are more than welcome to access our Business Referral List and obtain a referral for virtually anything ... from Childcare, Maids and Cleaning Professionals to Moving and Storage Companies.

History of the Business

Sample Concierge was formed in January 1999 in Sample City by two equal partners, John and Karen Smith, who hold equal shares in the company. After reading an article in Entrepreneur Magazine and searching the Internet it was discovered that Sample City had no corporate concierge company. They realized that John's sales and marketing experience combined with Karen's meeting and event-planning talent would make them the perfect team. They came up with a concierge service that targets both individual residents and area companies.

Founder(s) of the Business

The combined talent of the two partners John and Karen creates the uniqueness of this service. John has been in the sales and marketing and customer service fields for over 20 years and Karen has worked as a meeting planner for over 15 years, and has planned all types of meetings, events and exhibits across the country.

Management & Operations

John currently runs the business. He is also responsible for the sales and marketing of the company and is responsible for all the financial matters. Karen runs the operations. William Douglas is the company's accountant and bookkeeper. There are 2 full time errand drivers, 3 part time drivers, a night operations manager and an in-office administrative assistant.

Partners are allowed 2 weeks vacation, just not at the same time. Partners can expect a salary once the company begins to show a profit. Employees will be hired as needed. The partners prior to the hiring of the first employee will establish an employee handbook and benefit plan.

Regulations & Licensing

No licensing is required. Liability insurance is being looked into. Meeting Insurance is obtained on a meeting by meeting basis. Both Service Vendors and Members sign a basic liability contract when they sign on.

Objectives

It is Sample Concierge's objective to be able to meet its expenses by the end of August 1999. It is expected to show a profit by January 2000. In order to do this we will market the business through our 2 websites as well as direct-mail campaigns. Furthermore, we will obtain corporate clients by cold-calling various human relations departments, networking events and mailings.

SERVICE

Service Description

Sample Concierge is a one-stop shop designed to provide customers with an array of services. These include errand service, personal shopping, travel assistance, relocation services, meeting and event planning and our business referral service.

Related Products

It is not our intention to sell specific products, however, we will promote companies that offer various services and products that we feel our clients will value.

MARKETING

Objectives & Strategies

Sample Concierge has set its marketing objectives by targeting the human resources departments of area companies. An aggressive direct mail campaign as well as direct telephone calls to area companies will be used. Advertisements will be placed in local newspapers and magazines. A press release will be mailed out to all area media agencies. Finally, partners will attend as many Sample City Chamber of Commerce networking functions as possible to network with area company representatives.

Unique Selling Advantage

Sample Concierge is available whenever the client needs us.... our errand service is here 24 hours a day, 7 days a week via fax, telephone and e-mail.

Channels of Distribution

Sample Concierge intends to utilize its wide network of independent contractors to produce its services. The owners have obtained a written agreement from each service vendor that they will provide the various services and give Sample Concierge a 10% commission on each sale.

Pricing

Sample Concierge offers a yearly membership fee that ranges from $200 to $1,500 per year depending upon the type of package, number of employees and services required. Clients are also charged an hourly rate for our errand and personal shopping service. Meeting and event planning is quoted on a per event basis and depends on the type of event, how many people, location, and how long it will take to put the function together for the client.   Service vendors also give Sample Concierge a 10% commission.

Table 2

COMPANY	Commissions	% Variation from Market
Sample Errand Co.	10% - 15%	10% - 15%
Sample Concierge Co.	7% to 10%	7% to 10%

ADVERTISING

Advertising will concentrate on print advertising in the yellow pages, various magazines, newspapers and direct mail. The advertising budget will be 4% of the gross sales in the first and second year. The percentage increases to 6% thereafter.

Table 3

ADVERTISING

Type of Media	January	February	March	April
Yellow Pages	$412	$412	$412	$412
Business Leader Magazine	0	1,200	1,200	1,200
The Sample City Times	800	800	800	800
Direct Mail	500	500	500	500
TOTAL SPENDING	$6,100	$2,300	$2,300	$2,300

Publicity & Public Relations

Sample Concierge will send out a press release to all the local media agencies. At present, no budget has been allocated to public relations since it will be done by the owners through networking.

FINANCES

Start-Up Costs

An initial investment will be required in order for Sample Concierge to commence business. A budget of the company's required resources has been compiled in the following table.

The following numbers are not accurate representations of the current market and are for demonstration purposes only.

Table 4

START-UP COSTS

COST	AMOUNT
Salaries for two individuals	$50,000
Furniture and Equipment	$5,000
Rent for 3 months	$1,500
Utilities	$5,000
Legal and Professional Fees	$10,000
Advertising and Promotions	$10,000
Stationary, Brochures, etc..	$2,000
Consultants	$500
Insurance	$1,000
Research and development	$400
Miscellaneous	$1,000
TOTAL START-UP COSTS	$85,400

Sources & Uses of Capital

In order for Sample Concierge to successfully start operations, an total investment of $115,000 will be needed. The owners will each contribute $20,000 of their own money and will require an additional $75,000 from a lender. The business will require a 3-year loan that will be repaid in monthly installments

Table 5

SOURCES AND USES OF CAPITAL

SOURCES

Business Loan	$75,000
Owner Investment	$40,000
TOTAL SOURCES	$115,000

USES

Start up Costs	$85,400
working capital	$10,000
Reserve for contingencies	$20,000
TOTAL USES	$115,400

Opportunity

"This American system of ours ... call it Americanism, call it capitalism, call it what you like, gives to each and every one of us a great opportunity if we only seize it with both hands and make the most of it."

Al Capone

I couldn't resist ending this book with the above quote considering the notoriety of its author.

If any wish to contact me I can be reached through my company Triangle Concierge International. The email address is kgiovanni@triangleconcierge.com

Good luck!